ENCYCLOPEDIA OF ART
FOR YOUNG PEOPLE

The Renaissance

Tony Allan

CHELSEA HOUSE
PUBLISHERS
An imprint of Infobase Publishing

Encyclopedia of Art for Young People: The Renaissance

Chelsea House
An imprint of Infobase Publishing
132 West 31st Street
New York NY 10001

ISBN-10: 0-7910-9471-5
ISBN-13: 978-0-7910-9471-6

Set ISBN: 978-0-7910-9477-8

Library of Congress Cataloging-in-Publication Data

Kwint, Marius.
Encyclopedia of art for young people / Marius Kwint, Iain Zaczek, Rachel A.H. Beckett. -- 1st ed.
p. cm.
Includes bibliographical references and index.

ISBN 978-0-7910-9477-8

1. Art--History--Juvenile literature. I. Zaczek, Iain. II. Beckett, Rachel A. H. III. Title.
N5308.K88 2007
703--dc22
2007031020

Chelsea House books are available at special discounts when purchased in bulk quantities for businesses, associations, institutions, or sales promotions. Please call our Special Sales Department in New York at (212) 967-8800 or (800) 322-8755.

You can find Chelsea House on the World Wide Web at **http://www.chelseahouse.com**

Series Editor: Marius Kwint

For The Brown Reference Group plc
Project Editor: Graham Bateman
Editor: Virginia Carter
Design: Steve McCurdy
Picture Research: Laila Torsun
Senior Managing Editor: Tim Cooke
Production: Alastair Gourlay, Maggie Copeland
Editorial Director: Lindsey Lowe

Printed in Singapore
10 9 8 7 6 5 4 3 2 1

All links and web addresses were checked and verified to be correct at the time of publication. Because of the dynamic nature of the web, some addresses and links may have changed since publication and may no longer be valid.

Contents

Introduction

The Renaissance was a time of high achievement in the arts that changed the face of painting forever. It created the idea of the great artist as a star attraction whose name was internationally known and whose services kings, princes, and popes vied to attract. Its leading talents mastered a new way of looking at the world, learning to create a realistic image of what they saw about them. In doing so, they produced works that celebrated the natural universe and the splendors of the people who inhabited it, developing a relatively human frame of reference that contrasted with the God-centered viewpoint of the medieval artists who had gone before.

The change was less marked in sculpture, where a realistic tradition had already developed in the High Middle Ages (c.1000–1300). The craftsmen who carved the leaves of Southwell Minster in 13th-century England or the statues in Germany's Naumburg Cathedral had little to learn about capturing the outward appearance of things. Most of the advances made in sculpture in Renaissance times were as a result of a better understanding of anatomy and greater skill in depicting figures in motion.

In painting, though, there was a clear break with the past. The most important advance lay in the mastery of perspective, which enabled artists to create an illusion of depth in their works. Once paintings entered this third dimension, a new world of spatial composition opened up. There were technical advances too, such as the introduction of oil-based paints and woodcut engravings, both from about 1400 on.

The conquest of perspective was achieved in separate ways in different parts of Europe. In Italy scholars approached the question theoretically, working out the scientific rules underlying the problem, sometimes using mathematics. Painters in Florence and Rome then set about putting their findings to the test. One, Paolo Uccello, sometimes stayed up all night working out correct vanishing points; when his wife called him to bed, he would simply say, "Oh, what a lovely thing perspective is!"

In the Flanders region of northeastern Europe, meanwhile, artists such as Jan van Eyck arrived at similar solutions by means of observation alone. They learned from earlier generations of miniaturists who had sought to capture the appearance of things through trial and error.

By about 1520 almost all the great theoretical challenges had been resolved, and painting reached a peak in the hands of such masters as Leonardo da Vinci and Michelangelo, Raphael and Albrecht Dürer. A new problem then arose of what to do next.

A fresh generation of artists sought a solution in Mannerism, exploring the possibilities of lopsided compositions and contorted figures in place of the High Renaissance's perfect balance. The restless artistic spirit needed to press on once more, unhappy to repeat set formulae—however perfect they might seem to be.

STRUCTURE OF THE BOOK

The Renaissance opens with a Time Line that sets the artistic achievements discussed in the book against the wider context of events in world history. There follows a series of chapters covering in chronological sequence the development of European art from the 14th to the 16th centuries.

The four fully illustrated chapters contain themed feature spreads and boxes in the following categories:

Inside the Artist—highlights the main achievements of a particular artist or gives more information about the life and work of an artist profiled elsewhere in the book. For example, Albrecht Dürer, pages 68 to 69.

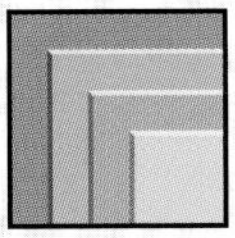

Schools and Movements—gives information about the characteristics of artistic schools, movements, or associated groups of artists. For example, The Bruges School, page 56.

Tools and Techniques—describes specific artistic techniques or materials. For example, Chiaroscuro, page 79.

Masterpiece—analyzes a particular work. For example, Botticelli's *Primavera*, page 39.

Connections—draws attention to stylistic influences among cultures or individual artists, or gives historical context to subjects dealt with elsewhere in the text. For example, "Sacred Conversation," page 18.

Where the text relates to topics discussed elsewhere in the book, cross references are given at the foot of the page. A glossary of specialized terms used is provided on pages 90 to 92, while to aid your research, Further References (books and Web sites) are listed on page 93. The index can be found on pages 94 to 96.

Time Line

The Art World

1337	Death of Giotto.
c.1400	Oil painting first appears. Woodcut prints are introduced in Germany around this time.
1401	Ghiberti wins a competition to design new doors for the Baptistery in Florence.
1428/29	Death of Masaccio.
c.1430	Luca della Robbia applies potters' lead glazes to terra-cotta sculptures to produce colored works. In Germany the first copperplate engravings date from about this time.
1431	Donatello arrives in Rome and devotes himself to the study of classical antiquities.
1432	Jan van Eyck: *Adoration of the Lamb*.
1435	Leon Battista Alberti explains the rules of perspective in his monograph *On Painting*.
c.1440	Donatello: *David*.
1441	Jan van Eyck dies.
1444	Witz: *Miraculous Draft of Fishes*.
1449	Fra Angelico is elected prior of the convent of Fiesole outside Florence.
1450	Rogier van der Weyden travels to Rome and Florence.
c.1452	Piero della Francesca begins his frescoes for the church of St. Francis in Arezzo.
c.1455	Giovanni Bellini joins a family workshop that will become the training ground for many painters of the Venetian School.
c.1460	Mantegna develops his "stony manner"; he works on his fresco for the ceiling of the Camera Picta at the Palazzo Ducale in Mantua from 1465–74.
1475–76	Hugo van der Goes: Portinari Altarpiece.
1482	Death of van der Goes.
c.1482	Botticelli: *Primavera*.
1500	Raphael enters the workshop of Perugino in Florence.
c.1504	Michelangelo: *David*.

The World

1337	The Hundred Years' War breaks out between England and France.
1347–48	The Black Death reduces the population of western Europe by as much as one-third.
1354	The Ottoman Turks invade the Gallipoli Peninsula, establishing a foothold in Europe.
1378	Gian Galeazzo Visconti comes to power in Milan. Before his death in 1402 he will make Milan the greatest power in northern Italy.
1378	Start of the Great Schism in the Catholic Church: Rival popes in Avignon and Rome denounce one another.
1381	Venice wins the War of Chioggia against Genoa, leaving it undisputed master of trade with the Eastern Mediterranean region.
1405	The Venetian army occupies the cities of Padua, Verona, and Vicenza in an attempt to overthrow the Carrara and Visconti dynasties.
1417	The Council of Constance ends the Great Schism. Martin V is elected pope, ruling the Church from Rome.
1418	Portugal's Prince Henry the Navigator launches the first sea voyages of the Age of Exploration.
1434	The republic of Florence comes under the control of the Medici banking family, led by Cosimo de' Medici, a patron of the arts.
c.1450	Johannes Gutenberg introduces movable-type printing to Europe, setting up a printing press in the German city of Mainz.
1450	The Sforza family takes power in Milan.
1453	The Ottoman Turks conquer Constantinople, bringing to an end more than 1,000 years of Byzantine civilization.
1465	Printing spreads across Italy from this date.
1478	The Pazzi Conspiracy in Florence fails to end the Medici family's control of the city.
1479	The Treaty of Constantinople ends Venice's 16-year war with the Ottoman Turks on unfavorable terms for the Italian city-state.

The Art World

1506	Leonardo da Vinci: *Mona Lisa*.
1506	*Laocoön and his Sons*, a lost Greek masterpiece, is unearthed in Rome, inspiring Michelangelo and other sculptors.
1508	Mabuse's visit to Italy helps start the Romanist tendency in Flemish art.
1510	Giorgione dies of plague in Venice.
c.1510	Bosch: *Garden of Earthly Delights*.
1512	Michelangelo: Sistine Chapel ceiling, Rome.
1514	Raphael succeeds Bramante as principal architect of St. Peter's Basilica in Rome.
c.1515	Grünewald: Isenheim Altarpiece.
1518	Pontormo: *Madonna and Child with Saints*, (often called the first Mannerist painting).
1519	Leonardo da Vinci dies at Amboise in France.
1520	Death of Raphael.
1526	Holbein the Younger moves to England.
1528	Deaths of Dürer and Grünewald.
1530	Fiorentino is summoned to France by King Francis I and becomes the first leader of the School of Fontainebleau.
1533	Titian becomes court painter to the Holy Roman Emperor Charles V.
c.1535	Parmigianino: *Madonna with the Long Neck*.
1541	Michelangelo: *The Last Judgment*.
1552	Bruegel the Elder travels to Italy.
c.1555	The Flemish sculptor Jean de Boulogne settles in Florence, where he will become better known as Giambologna.
1564	Death of Michelangelo.
1569	Death of Bruegel the Elder.
1573	Veronese is summoned by the Inquisition to justify his *Feast in the House of Levi*.
1576	Death of Titian.
1588	Death of Veronese.
1594	Death of Tintoretto.

The World

1492	The death of Lorenzo de' Medici (Lorenzo the Magnificent) signals the end of Florence's golden age.
1494	Charles VIII of France invades Italy, starting an age of foreign military intervention in the affairs of the peninsula.
1495	The monk Savonarola imposes a puritan dictatorship on Florence that ends when he is burned at the stake three years later.
1499	Milan falls to Louis XII, Charles's successor as king of France.
1517	In Germany Martin Luther nails his 95 Theses to the church door in Wittenberg—an act that marks the start of the Reformation.
1525	In the Italian Wars, Francis I of France is defeated and captured at the Battle of Pavia. In future Spain rather than France will be the dominant foreign power in Italy.
1527	Troops of the Holy Roman Emperor Charles V sack Rome.
1535	Milan passes under Spanish rule.
1542	The Catholic Church establishes the Universal Inquisition to combat heresy.
1545	The pope summons the Council of Trent to reform the Catholic Church, setting in motion the movement known as the Counter-Reformation. The council continues to meet periodically until 1563.
1555	The Treaty of Augsburg ends years of religious war in Germany by specifying that each German state shall adopt the faith—Catholic or Protestant—of its ruler.
1556	Philip II, a fervent supporter of the Catholic cause, becomes king of Spain on the abdication of his father Charles V.
1562	Religious war erupts in France against Protestant Huguenot rebels. The struggle continues, with breaks, until 1598.
1568	Revolt against Spanish rule breaks out in the Netherlands.
1570	Venice loses Cyprus to the Ottoman Turks.

c.1300–1450

The Pre- and Early Renaissance

The Renaissance was a time of cultural ferment. Although its impact was not limited to painting and sculpture, its effect on both was spectacular. The discoveries made in its course—a new realism in depicting objects and people, rules of perspective, fresh ways of handling depth and form—ushered in a new, naturalistic style that dominated the visual arts until the late 19th century.

The word "renaissance," meaning a rebirth, was only applied to the age by scholars 400 years later. Yet the idea was not strange to people of the time. What was being reborn, in their view, was a knowledge of classical Greece and Rome. Although the Renaissance eventually made its presence felt all across Europe, its first home was Italy. Awareness of past glories was particularly strong there, for the relics of ancient Rome lay all around. Even so, the peninsula at first sight seemed an unlikely setting for a cultural revival, since its medieval history had been particularly violent.

A DIVIDED LAND

In the 13th century the land was devastated by wars between the Holy Roman emperors—German monarchs claiming control over Italy—and the popes, who saw themselves as secular Italian rulers as well as spiritual heads of the Catholic Church. In 1305 the popes abandoned Rome for Avignon in southern France, and from 1373 to 1442 there were separate popes in Avignon and Rome. Italy fragmented among five major powers centered on Naples in the south, the Papal States in the center, Milan to the north, Venice to the east, and Florence to the west.

Other, smaller powers also found a place on the stage, for Renaissance Italy was a land of city-states, each ruling over a rural hinterland. Many were controlled by ruling families, and all were engaged in a perpetual struggle to survive and expand their lands.

For all its conflicts and violence, this divided land had features that proved highly stimulating for artistic creativity. Italy was an urban society; its towns and cities were more developed than any in Europe. Feudalism, which had seen power and wealth concentrated in the hands of barons living on landed estates, was largely confined to the south.

SOCIAL CHANGE

Within the towns, new social forces came to the fore that proved beneficial for painters and sculptors. A new wealthy middle class of bankers, merchants, and lawyers were only too happy to patronize individuals of talent. It helped that such people showed intense local patriotism, seeking to beautify the streets and churches of their own city so as to outshine those of its rivals.

The new social freedoms of the post-feudal world inevitably created a fresh intellectual atmosphere. In the Middle Ages, learning had been the exclusive preserve of the Church. That situation changed in Renaissance times. While still for the most part deeply pious, many wealthy townspeople sought a secular education for their children, wishing to prepare them for careers in business or the law rather than as priests. The intellectual movement known as humanism was born among the teachers they employed, and its chief breeding grounds were the universities, in which the classical heritage of Greece and Rome was passed on. Painters and sculptors followed the scholars' example and learned from the artistic heritage of the ancient world.

Before the Renaissance, art was largely anonymous, as in this 12th-century icon painting of the Archangel Gabriel.

The Byzantine tradition

The wind of change sweeping the peninsula soon made itself felt in the visual arts. Renaissance painting emerged out of the Byzantine tradition of formal, two-dimensional figures delineated against a decorative background, often of gold leaf. In medieval times painting was a craft whose skills were passed down from masters to apprentices. The works they produced were often beautiful and finely done, but they were also derivative. Individuality was not encouraged—the aim of painting and sculpture was to express the unchanging truths of religion. Young artists had little incentive to regard the world afresh. The result was a largely anonymous body of art whose greatest practitioners rarely signed their works or left their names to posterity.

A new style of sculpture

A new mood first made itself felt in sculpture. Nicola and Giovanni Pisano, a father and son from Tuscany, had been the first to abandon Byzantine models in favor of a more realistic style. Nicola, who was dead by 1284, worked under the influence of classical statuary. Giovanni (c.1245/50–1314/19) looked more to France, where fresh observation from nature had been making itself felt within the established Gothic style.

The innovations of the Pisanos were soon imitated across Italy, and they contributed to a similar revolution in painting. Florence was to be the home of the new style, and there its best-known precursor was Cimabue (c.1240–?1302). He continued to work within the

Schools and Movements

Humanism

Humanism was an intellectual movement that affected scholarship and education as well as the fine arts, first in Italy and then elsewhere in Europe from the late 14th century onward. The word derives from the Latin *studia humanitatis*, meaning "studies of humankind," and the first humanists were teachers of such subjects as rhetoric and law. Whereas education in earlier days had fallen under the influence of the Church, the humanists looked to other authorities, particularly classical Greece and Rome, for a more worldly form of learning.

From the start there were close contacts between artists and humanists. The Sienese painter Simone Martini (c.1284–1344) was a friend of the Italian poet and scholar Petrarch (1304–74). He painted a portrait (now lost) of Laura, the subject of Petrarch's finest love poetry. At the poet's behest, he also illustrated a copy of the works of the great Roman poet Virgil. In the longer term humanism helped create a secular audience for painting to complement the religious art patronized by the Church. The Renaissance taste for scenes from classical mythology could never have developed without its influence.

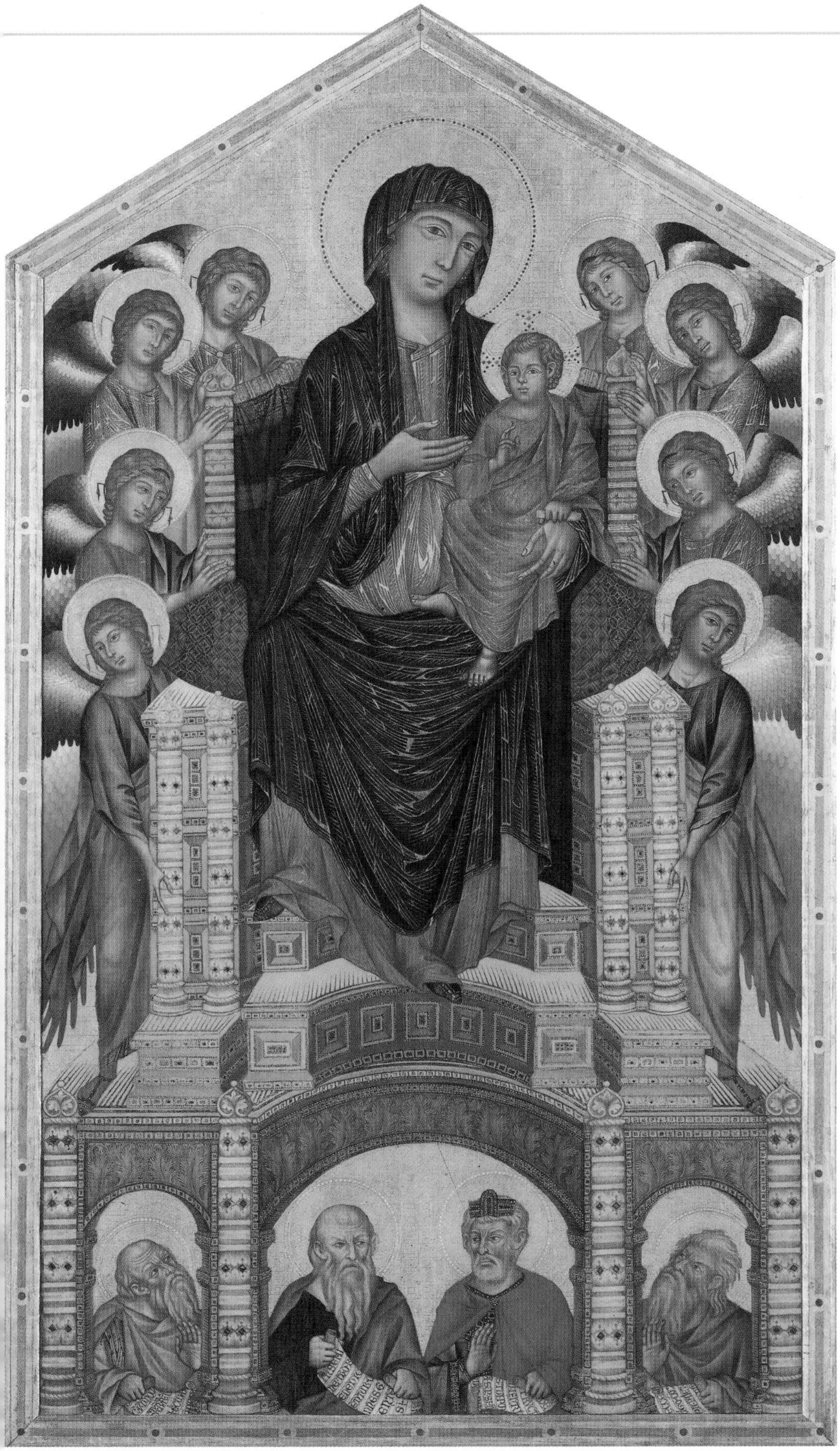

In his **Santa Trinita Madonna** *Cimabue portrayed the subject in a three-dimensional and realistic way.*

Byzantine tradition, but he brought a statuesque quality to later works such as the *Santa Trinita Madonna* (c.1260/80), which is now in the Uffizi Gallery in Florence, that foreshadowed later Renaissance developments.

Duccio and Giotto

The masters of the next generation made crucial breakthroughs without which Renaissance art would not have been able to develop. In Siena Duccio di Buoninsegna (c.1255–1319) brought a new pathos and humanity to the established tradition. He excelled in the grouping of figures, as in his *Arrest of Christ* (1311)—one of a series of scenes from the life of Christ painted to decorate the back of the altarpiece of Siena Cathedral. The eloquence of his compositions introduced a sense of human drama that was missing in the static, God-centered world of classic Byzantine art.

Even so, Duccio's figures remained relatively two-dimensional: The art critic Bernard Berenson (1865–1959) dismissed them as appearing to be "manufactured of tissue paper." In contrast, Berenson claimed, Duccio's younger Florentine contemporary Giotto (c.1270–1337) gave his figures "tactile values," the sense that the spectator could reach out and touch them.

Almost from his own time Giotto, a peasant's son from the Florence area with a natural talent, was seen as the true creator of the new art. Giotto's teacher may have been Cimabue. A story claims that he stumbled on the younger man's talent by chance: While making a journey, he happened to notice a shepherd scratching pictures of his sheep with a sharpened stone on a rock. He took the stranger as an apprentice into his studio, where Giotto's skills quickly blossomed. Once, the story goes, he painted a fly on the nose of a painted figure that was so lifelike that Cimabue tried to brush it off.

The best known of the tales about Giotto similarly emphasizes his self-confidence and natural talent. It relates how he demonstrated his draftsmanship to a messenger sent by the pope to verify his skill, by drawing a perfect circle in red paint. Impressed by the gesture, the pope summoned him to Rome, where he carried out many important commissions.

Completed in 1311, Duccio's Maestà *was a huge two-sided altarpiece for Siena Cathedral. This scene from one of the reverse panels tells the story of The Arrest of Christ.*

CONNECTIONS

Tactile Values

The term "tactile values" was coined by art critic Bernard Berenson to describe the illusion of tangibility produced by the naturalistic painting style of the Renaissance masters. For Berenson, the tactile sense stimulated by their ability to capture three-dimensional reality with the aid of advances in perspective and knowledge of human anatomy was their greatest contribution to the development of art. "Tactile values and movement," he wrote, "are the essential qualities in the figure arts, and no figure-painting is real ... unless it conveys ideated sensations of touch and movement." Once widely used, the term fell out of fashion in art-historical circles as art itself became less representational in the course of the 20th century.

Many other patrons followed the papal example, and Giotto subsequently traveled from city to city to decorate the walls of churches, monasteries, and private chapels. He found his way to Assisi, Pisa, Ferrara, Urbino, Arrezzo,

Naples, Rimini, Padua, Milan, and other Italian cities, as well as to Avignon in southern France. In so doing, he set a pattern that was followed by later Renaissance masters who mostly lived peripatetic lives, working for a succession of wealthy patrons who competed to employ their talents.

At the end of his life Giotto returned to his native Florence to supervise work on the city's cathedral. Here too he established a precedent—

Giotto's **Lamentation Over the Dead Christ,** *1303–06, is one of the frescoes he painted on the upper walls of the Arena Chapel in Padua.*

other masters including Leonardo da Vinci (1452–1519) and Michelangelo (1475–1564) would later also turn their hand to architecture and engineering as well as to painting and sculpture.

As an artist Giotto was admired above all for his naturalism, which contrasted markedly with the stylized art of the preceding age. His draftsmanship was particularly commended, as the story of the perfect circle would suggest. In more recent times he has retained his position of preeminence, praised for the simplicity of his compositions and his ability to convey emotion as well as the solidity of his figures and the achievement of a three-dimensional effect in portraying form and space.

 See also: The High Renaissance in Italy **28–49;** The Late Renaissance and Mannerism **70–89**

SCHOOLS AND MOVEMENTS

The Sienese School

In the early decades of the Renaissance in Italy, the Tuscan city of Siena rivaled Florence, just 30 miles (50 km) to the north, as a center for new directions in art. Local differences being what they were, however, the two near-neighbors developed in very different ways. Whereas Florence took its lead from Giotto, who encouraged muscular experimentation with form, Siena followed Duccio, who remained much closer to the Byzantine tradition. Following his example, his successors proved less interested in formal experimentation than the Florentine artists, concentrating instead on producing works of extraordinary beauty and refinement in the existing tradition, while nonetheless borrowing certain elements of the new realism from their northern contemporaries.

About 30 years younger than Duccio, Simone Martini (c.1284–1344) kept the golden background of Byzantine painting for some of his works, but brought a fresh feeling for elegance and grace, distinguished by a taste for slender bodies and the play of flowing drapery. Martini's contemporaries, the Lorenzetti brothers, worked closer to the Florentine tradition. The younger of the two, Ambrogio (fl.1319–48), between 1337 and 1339 painted an extraordinary series of frescoes in the Town Hall of Siena on the theme of good and bad government that were stylistically in advance of anything painted in Italy for the next half-century.

Ambrogio and his brother Pietro (fl.1320–45) both died in 1348 of the Black Death, which reduced the population of Siena from about 100,000 to about 13,000. The disaster effectively put an end to the city's artistic influence—it never regained the prominence it had acquired in the Renaissance's early stages.

Il Buon Governo *(Good Government),1337–39, one of Ambrogio Lorenzetti's frescoes that decorates the interior of the east wall of the Town Hall in Siena.*

A period of retrenchment

Giotto died in 1337, but his work lived on to influence an entire generation of Italian painters. Yet a century went by before Renaissance art emerged in its full splendor. In the decades after his death, some of the most interesting work was done in Siena, whose artists learned from his work but still owed much to the Byzantine tradition. Painters elsewhere were seduced by the grace and elegance of the International Gothic style popular at the time in the lands north of the Alps, well exemplified in the *Madonna of the Rose Garden* (c.1420) by Paduan artist Stefano da Zevio (c.1375–?1438). For Berenson, a champion of Giotto's muscular realism, such work was little more than decoration: "pretty faces, pretty color, pretty clothes, and trivial action."

One reason for the relatively slow take-up of Giotto's naturalism lay in the fact that exceptional talent was needed to bridge the gap between his work and the fluency of the High Renaissance masters that would come later. For all Giotto's genius, the faces of his personages remained masklike, and the integration of individual figures with one another and with the background was still incomplete. Equally important was the Black Death, which devastated Italy in 1347 and 1348, just a decade after Giotto's death. The epidemic not only killed many talented artists but also left in its wake a darkened mood of pessimism and religious fervor that was not conducive to experimentation and new beginnings. The economic disruption caused by the plague also affected the opportunities for new commissions.

Connections

Quattrocento

Literally meaning "400" in Italian and short for *mille quattrocento*, or 1400, the term quattrocento has long been applied by art historians to works produced in Italy in the 15th century. As such, it is virtually synonymous with "Early Renaissance," at least as applied to the Italian school. Sometimes the word carries an implied value judgment—the Pre-Raphaelite painters of 19th-century England, for instance, used it to distinguish the simpler and, in their view, purer works of the earlier period from the more sophisticated products of the Late Renaissance.

Fra Angelico

Talented artists worked in Florence in Giotto's wake, but the next true master to emerge from the city was not born until 50 years after his death. Fra Giovanni ("Brother John") was a Dominican friar, and the emphasis of his work was delicate and spiritual. Indeed, the saints and madonnas that he painted were so

ECCE VIRGO CONCIPIET 7 PARIET FILIVM 7 VOCABIT NOMEN EIVS EMANVL. YSA.VI.C
ECCE CONCIPIES INVTERO 7 PARIES FILIVM 7 VOCABIS NOMEN EI9 IHESVM. LVCE. I. C.
REGES TARSIS 7 INSVLE MVNERA OFFERET REGES ARABV 7 SABBA DONA ADVCET. PS. LXXI. C

graceful and refined that he became known to his contemporaries as Fra Giovanni Angelico ("the angelic Brother John"), and is now remembered as Fra Angelico (c.1395–1455).

Although his figures have rounded forms that would not have been possible without Giotto, Fra Angelico worked firmly in the Sienese tradition of elegance and refinement. In his case the motivation

Fra Angelico's* Annunciation*, c.1450, painted for St. Mark's Convent, Florence.

Gozzoli's The Journey of the Magi *(detail shown) is one of three wall frescoes painted for the Medici-Riccardi Palace in Florence. Gozzoli adapted his style to meet the demands of his patrons—in these frescoes he used rich colors that reflected the taste of Piero de' Medici.*

Connections

"Sacred Conversation"

Sacra conversazione—literally, "sacred conversation"—is a term used by art historians to describe paintings showing the Virgin Mary and infant Jesus surrounded by saints. In earlier art the Madonna and child had usually been depicted separately from the saints, who were restricted to the outside panels of a triptych. Fra Angelico (c.1395–1455) introduced the idea of showing the various characters interacting within a single panel or canvas. Other artists who adopted the form included Fra Filippo Lippi (c.1406–69), Andrea Mantegna (c.1431–1506), Piero della Francesca (c.1415–92), and Giovanni Bellini (c.1400–70/71).

behind the works was largely spiritual—he is said never to have taken up his paintbrushes without saying a prayer. A modest man, he reportedly turned down the chance to become archbishop of Florence in favor of his friend and fellow monk, the future Saint Antoninus. His work, done mostly for monasteries and churches, was marked by serenity and delicate coloration, along with static compositions suitable for contemplation. He passed on his love of color to his pupil Benozzo Gozzoli (c.1421–97), who used it to gorgeous effect in purely secular works such as *The Journey of the Magi* (1459–61), which shows members of Florence's ruling Medici family in the guise of the Biblical wise men.

 See also: The High Renaissance in Italy **28–49**

Masaccio

Giotto's true heir was a contemporary of Fra Angelico's, born Tommasso di Ser Giovanni di Mone in a village in the Arno Valley outside Florence. He found fame as Masaccio (1401–28/29), a nickname derived from his Christian name Tommasso that meant approximately "Grungy Tom," reflecting his disdain for cleanliness and neat dressing. Instead, he poured all his considerable energy into his art, with the result that during his short lifetime he revolutionized painting, setting it on the course of heightened naturalism that was to be the hallmark of the High Renaissance.

Masaccio seems to have reacted against the cult of prettiness associated with the International Gothic style, championed at the time in Florence by the painter Gentile da Fabriano (c.1385–1427). He favored an austere heroic style marked by concentrated dramatic power and solidity of form. In this last respect he outdid even Giotto, employing a knowledge of perspective and foreshortening that was more sophisticated than that of the earlier master, and so bringing painting closer to capturing real life.

Masaccio left relatively little work, but he nonetheless won an enduring reputation as a painter's painter. Generations of artists, among them all the great Renaissance masters, trooped to the Brancacci Chapel of the Carmelite Church in Florence, where his greatest masterpieces are preserved. Had he lived longer, he might have become one of the most famous of them all. As it was, he passed on the baton to successors such

Masaccio's fresco **Raising of the Son of Theophilus,** *1426–27, at Santa Maria del Carmine, Florence, included important new ideas such as well-proportioned figures and the use of perspective.*

TOOLS AND TECHNIQUES

The Discovery of Perspective

One of the most vital breakthroughs of the Early Renaissance lay in the mastery of perspective, which permitted painters to create a three-dimensional illusion of depth on a two-dimensional picture surface. The first man to spell out its laws was the Florentine architect and sculptor Filippo Brunelleschi (1377–1446), who conducted optical experiments to show why objects closer to the viewer seem larger than those farther away.

His follower Leon Battista Alberti (1404–72) continued Brunelleschi's work, spelling out in his treatise *On Painting* (1435) formulae by which artists could calculate the proportional differences in size of painted figures in relation to their distance from the viewer. Alberti also demonstrated how the horizontal planes of a picture should converge at a so-called vanishing point deep within the scene.

The painter who probably applied himself most single-mindedly to mastering the new principles was Paolo Uccello (c.1397–1475), whose wife used to complain that he was more interested in perspective than he was in her. Yet for all their charm, his works lack the fluency of the greatest masters because of their rigid adherence to theory.

Mastery of depth in painting in fact involved much more than the mere application of scientific principles, and was only truly achieved when High Renaissance artists added to a mastery of linear perspective and foreshortening a knowledge of how to convey distance by effects of light and shade.

as Andrea del Castagno (c.1418–57), another short-lived Florentine who grew up under the influence of Masaccio's studied realism.

THE SCULPTOR DONATELLO

For talent and dramatic power, Masaccio's only real rival was a sculptor. Born in Florence a decade or so earlier, Donatello (c.1386–1466) used his long life to make himself the model of the Renaissance artist. On the one hand, he had an intellectual cast of mind that led him to immerse himself in the theoretical works of his friend Filippo Brunelleschi (1377–1446), so becoming an early

At least two vanishing points, both focusing on the rearing horse in the foreground, can be seen in Uccello's* Battle of San Romano*, c.1450s.

champion of perspective. In a series of low reliefs sculpted from about 1417 on he developed a sense of pictorial space well beyond anything that painters had achieved by that time. He also struggled constantly to animate his figures through expression and movement, reportedly muttering at them as he worked, "Speak, damn you, speak!"

Then again, he had a passion for the antique, spending two years in Rome in the 1430s doing little but studying classical art. According to biographer Giorgio Vasari (1511–74), his subsequent work was considered "nearer what was done by the ancient Greeks and Romans than that of any other artist."

Most importantly of all, he used the techniques of naturalism pioneered in the early Renaissance to establish a new ideal of human potential. In statues like his *David* (c.1440s) or *Saint George* (c.1420), now in the Bargello in Florence, he created a fresh standard of masculine beauty. Often literally larger than life, his figures represented aspirational images of what Berenson called "the type of human being most likely to win the day in the combat of human forces." In his work observation of nature came together with a sense of the sublime to mark the emergence of the Renaissance spirit in fully fledged form.

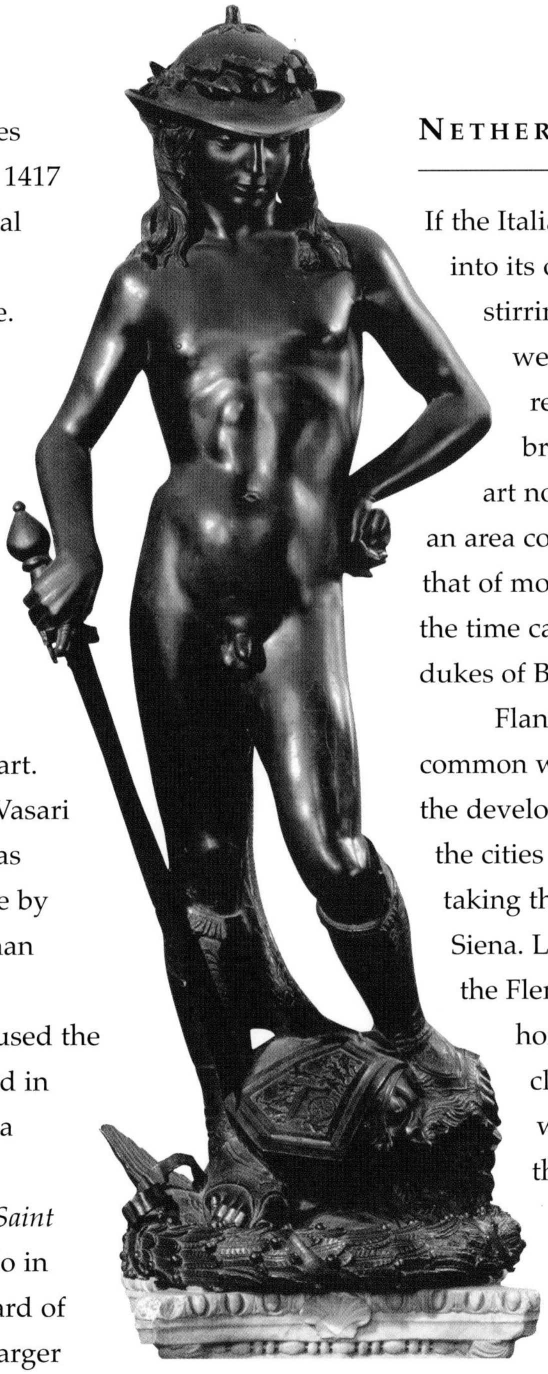

Among Donatello's works from his final years in Florence is the bronze statue* David, *c.1440s, which was unusual for its near nudity.

NETHERLANDISH STIRRINGS

If the Italian Renaissance really came into its own with Donatello, fresh stirrings elsewhere in Europe were also already producing remarkable results. The breeding ground for the new art north of the Alps was Flanders, an area coinciding approximately with that of modern-day Belgium, which at the time came under the rule of the dukes of Burgundy.

Flanders shared several features in common with northern Italy, above all in the development of an urban society, with the cities of Bruges, Ghent, and Tournai taking the place of Florence, Rome, and Siena. Like their Italian counterparts, the Flemish cities also provided a home for an emergent middle class who were found to be willing and able to patronize the arts.

Yet there were a number of differences, too. The Flemish cities may have had strong civic traditions, but they came under the rule of an aristocratic court that itself took the lead in championing talent. Then again, Flanders inherited a different artistic legacy; the example of classical antiquity was less important there than in the south, while the pull of Gothic art remained stronger.

A realist tradition in sculpture

The first true impulse to realism in the region came from sculpture, just as it had in Italy in the work of the Pisanos a century before. The pivotal figure in the north was Claus Sluter (c.1350–1405/6), who was born in the northern Netherlands and spent his career working for Philip II the Bold, Duke of Burgundy (1342–1404), first in Flanders and later in the Burgundian capital of Dijon. Sluter had his own antecedents in the form of the realistically minded German sculptor Peter Parler (c.1330–99) and the anonymous masters whose work can be seen in Naumburg Cathedral. Learning from their example, he created startlingly naturalistic figures that must have appeared all the more lifelike at the time for being painted in bright colors.

Connections

The Duchy of Burgundy

Centered on the Burgundy region of what is now east–central France, the duchy of Burgundy emerged as a European power in the late Middle Ages. It played a significant role in art history thanks to its acquisition of Flanders in 1384 as the result of a dynastic marriage. Flanders remained in Burgundian hands for almost a century until the death of Charles the Bold (1433–77).

In the intervening years the duchy rivalled its neighbor France in power and prestige. Its court, initially based at Dijon but in Flanders from about 1425, was famous for its lavish support of the arts, and with the dukes' encouragement painting flourished in the Flemish cities. Such 15th-century masters as the van Eycks, Robert Campin (c.1375–1444), Rogier van der Weyden (c.1399–1464), and Hugo van der Goes (c.1440–82) are sometimes collectively referred to as the "Burgundian School," although that term is now more often applied to a group of contemporary musicians and composers who also benefited from the dukes' patronage.

Campin and van Eyck

The path that Sluter blazed in sculpture was carried into painting by two early Netherlandish painters of contrasting genius. Controversy surrounds one, Robert Campin (c.1375–1444), who is now generally thought to have also been responsible for a body of work earlier attributed to an anonymous Master of Flémalle. Campin learned to give his figures a sculptural quality from studying Sluter's work. Campin's work combined realistic detail with a taste for dramatic, contorted figures and voluminous, heavily folded drapery. The atmosphere was dramatic, even expressionist.

In contrast, the art of Jan van Eyck (c.1390–1441) was contemplative and serene. As was often the case at the time, painting for him was a family business. One of his masterpieces, the multipaneled

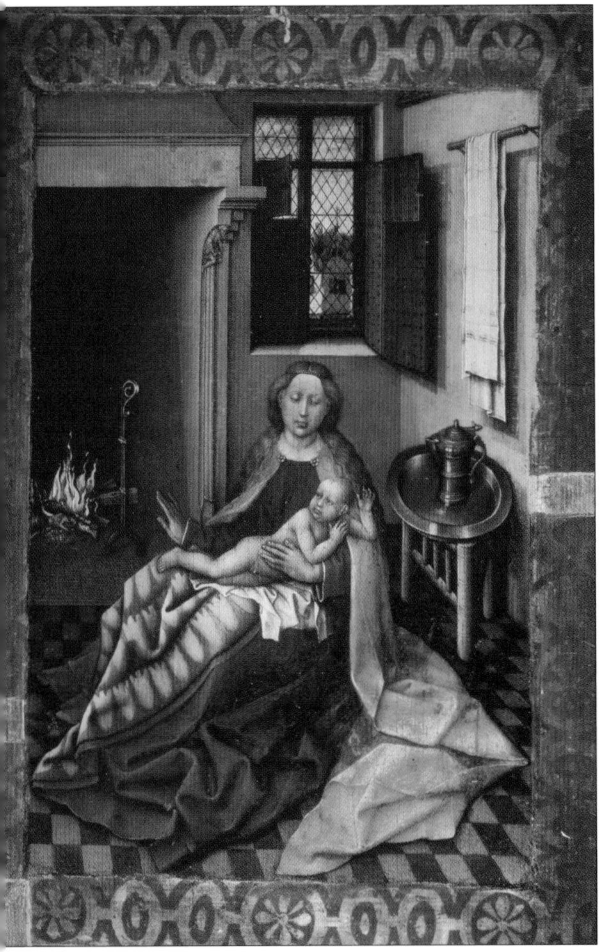

Virgin and Child by a Fireplace, ***the right wing of a diptych by Robert Campin realistically depicts details of everyday life.***

Adoration of the Lamb (1432) in Saint Bavo Cathedral, Ghent, bears an inscription indicating that the work was begun by his brother Hubert (c.1370–1426), about whom little is known.

What is certain is that Jan developed in his own painting a degree of realism unmatched by anything in Italy at the time. Yet he achieved his naturalism by an entirely different route from that taken by the Italian painters, employing none of the theoretical underpinning provided by the

TOOLS AND TECHNIQUES

Oil Painting

Before the Renaissance, artists generally made their own paints by grinding pigments derived from plants or minerals to a powder between two stones, then adding a liquid to create a paste. The preferred binding agent was egg yolk and white, which produced the paints known as tempera. The paint was then usually applied over a base of *gesso*—an Italian word meaning chalk, used to describe powdered calcium carbonate mixed with animal glue and applied to wooden panels as a primer.

From the 13th century on, however, some artists started replacing the egg with various types of oil, mostly linseed from the seeds of the flax plant. The resulting oil paints turned out to have several advantages over tempera. They were slow to dry, allowing artists to work on a given picture for weeks or months. They could be applied in thick layers, creating deeply saturated colors; in comparison, tempera works came to look washed out, almost like watercolors. In addition, the layers blended into one another, permitting subtle shadings of color.

At first oils were used for decoration, such as painting designs on shields, since they also had the advantage of being hard-wearing once dry. They came into widespread use in the fine arts only in the early 15th century.

Flemish painters pioneered the trend, particularly Jan van Eyck (c.1390–1441), sometimes called the "father of oil painting." He was also the first master to fully exploit the new medium's rich and glossy colors, applied in transparent layers, or "glazes," and to add glittering highlights with the aid of a pointed brush.

Renaissance scholars of Rome and Florence. Instead, he worked in the tradition of the medieval miniaturists, relying on focused observation and an intense attention to detail. By patient effort, van Eyck also achieved a mastery of light and of perspective that allowed him to create a completely convincing image of the world.

Among the delights of van Eyck's paintings are the landscapes that feature in the background of many of his works. A tradition of landscape painting had already established itself within the International Gothic tradition, notably in the work of the Limbourg brothers who prepared a celebrated Book of Hours—*Très Riches Heures*—for the Duke of Berry (1340–1416). Before long, scenes drawn from real locations began to appear. The first full-size panel painting to depict a recognizable vista is generally held to be the *Miraculous Draught of Fishes*, painted by the Swiss artist Konrad Witz (c.1400–44/46) in 1444. It shows Christ walking the shores of Lake Geneva, with Mount Salève in the background.

ROGIER VAN DER WEYDEN

The traditions of Campin and van Eyck were to come together in the work of another master of the early Netherlandish school, Rogier van der Weyden (c.1399–1464). He studied under Campin at Tournai, and early masterpieces such as the *Descent from the Cross* (c.1435, now in the Prado in Madrid) reflect Campin's taste for pathos and emotion, combined with a feeling for linear outline set against a background of gold that harks back to Gothic and Byzantine tradition.

Van der Weyden went on to enjoy a successful career as the official City Painter of Brussels. His later works continued to excel in expressing emotion, while also showing an attention to detail and a sensitive treatment of landscape that reflected the influence of van Eyck. In 1450 he traveled to Rome and Florence, where he learned from the early Renaissance masters while at the same time influencing a fresh generation of rising artists. Thus the Italian and Flemish traditions came together in shared admiration, with each continuing to retain a strong individual identity.

Opposite: In* The Virgin of Chancellor Rolin*, c.1435, Van Eyck shows his mastery in the representation of space. Nicolas Rolin, on the left, was chancellor to the Duchy of Burgundy from 1422 to 1457.

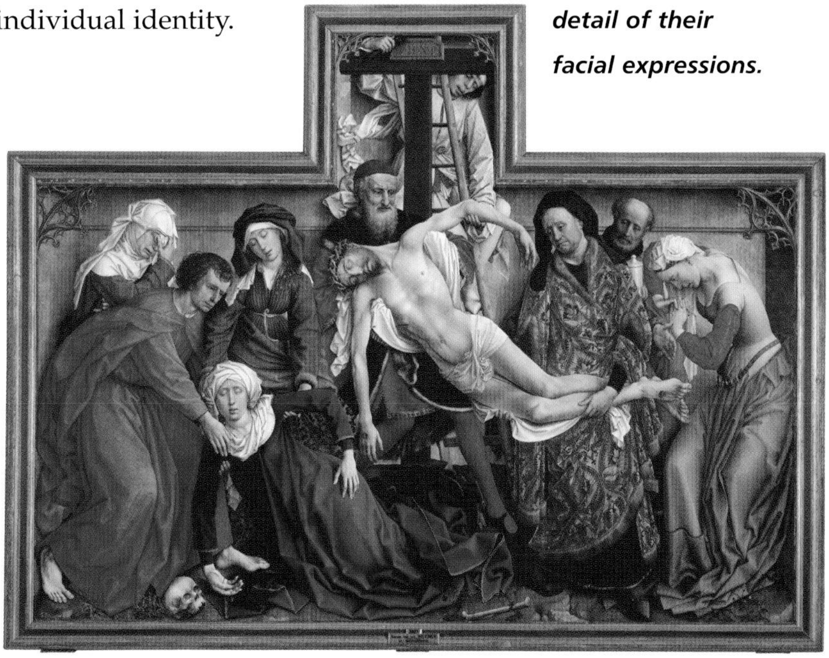

Van der Weyden's* Descent from the Cross*, c.1435, evokes intense emotion by the arrangement of figures and the detail of their facial expressions.

MASTERPIECE

The Gates of Paradise

In 1401 the merchant guild of Florence announced a competition to provide a pair of gilded bronze doors for the Baptistery. This distinctive, octagonal building, located next door to Florence Cathedral, was the oldest in the city, and it already had magnificent sculpted eastern doors made by Andrea Pisano (c.1290–1348/9) in the 1330s.

The new portal was designed to complement these doors on the north side of the building. Pisano's original doors were later relocated to the south side, where they can still be seen today.

A Bitter Contest

Some of the finest sculptors in Tuscany took part in the competition, which involved producing a relief of the biblical Sacrifice of Isaac. The names of seven of the competitors have been preserved, among them such talents as Jacopo della Quercia (1374/75–1438) and Filippo Brunelleschi (1377–1446), who was so disgusted when he failed to win the contest that he subsequently abandoned sculpture for architecture.

The judges eventually awarded the commission to Lorenzo Ghiberti (c.1380–1455). The 23-year-old Ghiberti thereby had an unrivaled opportunity to immortalize himself at a key time and place in Renaissance history.

Ghiberti labored on the task for the next 21 years, producing 28 bronze reliefs depicting biblical scenes. When the job was finally completed, he barely had time for a visit to Venice before he received a fresh commission for yet another set of doors—the third in all—to replace Pisano's work on the east side of the Baptistery.

This time Ghiberti was given the right to work to his own design, choosing to limit the number of relief panels to 10, five for each door. This work occupied him for another 27 years, reaching completion in 1452, just three years before his death.

This final set of doors is considered to be Ghiberti's masterpiece. In his reliefs the sculptor incorporated the latest notions of perspective as laid out theoretically by his one-time rival Brunelleschi—he even increased the effect by making the figures in the foreground more solid than those in the background. The bronzes, designed to appear like pictures in a frame, were richly gilded, further enhancing the magnificence of the effect.

Ghiberti had cast images of people, creatures, and buildings and made them completely lifelike, bringing realism, emotion, and drama to the stories of the Bible. Michelangelo said the doors were fit to serve as the gates of Paradise, and they remain one of the enduring masterpieces of Renaissance Florence.

Detail from the third panel of the right wing of Ghiberti's so-called Paradise Gates, telling the story of Joseph.

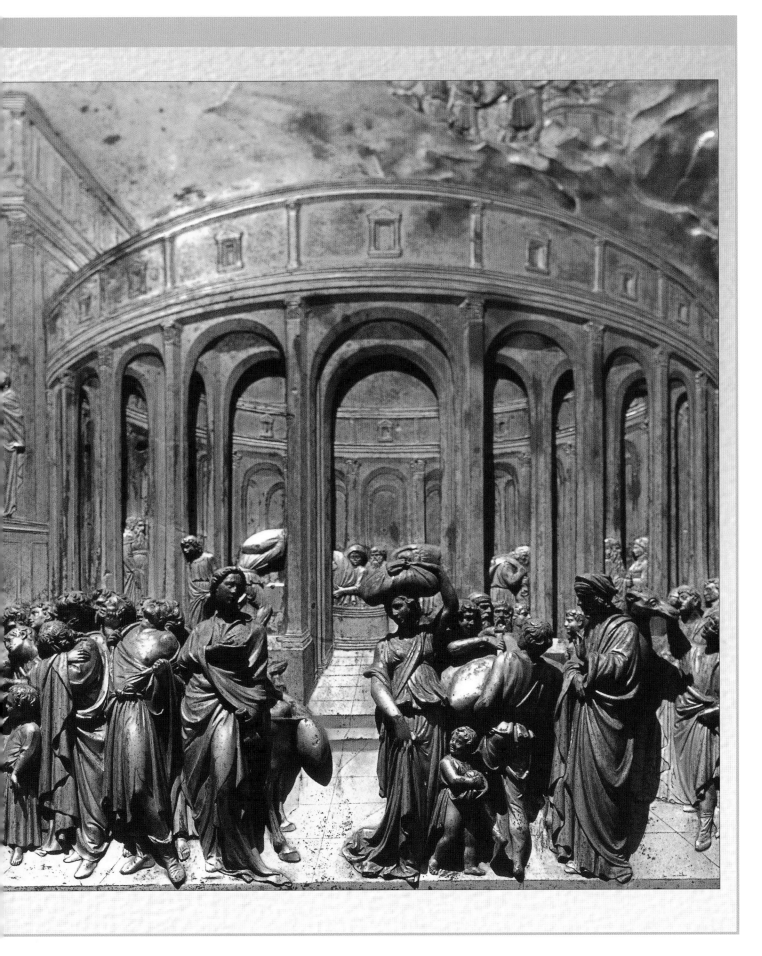

c.1450–1525

The High Renaissance in Italy

The rebirth of interest in classical antiquity that began in the 14th century reached its peak in Italy during the High Renaissance in the mid- to late 15th century. Characterized by harmony and balance, the art of painting had matured in terms of technical skill, imagination, and composition. The list of artistic geniuses from this time is unparalleled: Leonardo da Vinci, Raphael, Botticelli, Michelangelo—these towering giants are considered the greatest artists of all time.

The High Renaissance years in Italy, falling between about 1450 and 1525, were a time of artistic triumph and deepening political crisis. Art reached a pinnacle of achievement at a time when corruption and violence were on the rise and the threat of foreign military intervention loomed.

The story of the Pazzi Conspiracy, which rocked Florence in 1478, gives a flavor of the times. The Pazzi clan were banking rivals of Florence's ruling Medici family, and they had recently won the Vatican account from their competitors. With the knowledge of Pope Sixtus IV (1414–84), they conspired to kill Lorenzo de' Medici (1449–92) and his younger brother Giuliano (1453–78) and replace them with a nephew of the pope, whose recent appointment as archbishop of Pisa had been blocked by Lorenzo. The attack was carried out during Easter High Mass in Florence Cathedral. At the height of the ceremony, the conspirators—one a priest—cut down the 24-year-old Giuliano with 19 separate stab wounds as he knelt to pray.

Lorenzo was wounded but managed to take refuge in an inner room. Friends of the Medicis quickly rallied, and when the pope's nephew entered the ducal palace to take control of the city, he was confronted by Lorenzo's bodyguard, who hanged him from an upstairs window in his church robes, together with several other conspirators. The Florentine mob then set about avenging Giuliano; in the next few weeks 270 individuals suspected of association with the Pazzi family were hunted down and killed.

A new element was added to this world of intrigue and assassination when foreign powers started looking covetously at Italy's wealth. In 1494 Charles VIII of France (1470–98) used an old dynastic claim to the throne of Naples as an excuse for invading the peninsula. For the next 65 years or so competing powers turned Italy into a battleground, providing a backdrop of death and destruction for the work of such masters of world art as Leonardo da Vinci, Raphael, Michelangelo, and Titian.

A WORLD OF CONSPICUOUS DISPLAY

The careers of these artists were possible only because in the early years of the invasions much of the wealth of former times survived. Ruling elites like the Medicis lavished huge sums on the arts, providing an alternative, secular source of patronage to supplement the Church's need for altarpieces and other sacred works. In the High Renaissance years wealthy people competed for the services of the best artists, who lived wandering lives traveling from one royal or ducal court to another.

One result of the prevailing atmosphere of conspicuous display was that successful painters and sculptors enjoyed a newly enhanced status.

A portrait of Giuliano de' Medici by Botticelli (c.1478). The powerful Medici family was at the center of the political intrigue that characterized late 15th-century Italy.

Young artists still started their careers in the workshops of their elders as they had done in medieval times, but some of these established masters, such as Verrocchio in Florence or the Bellini family in Venice, now gained a reputation that stretched far beyond the confines of their own cities.

Such men no longer regarded themselves as simple artisans, as their predecessors had done. They dealt with

their aristocratic clients if not as equals, at least as people of consequence who deserved respect. Cosimo de' Medici (1389–1464), who dominated Florence from the 1430s to the 1460s, said of them, "One must treat these individuals of extraordinary genius as if they were celestial spirits, and not like beasts of burden." His successors took him at his word, and the painter and critic Giorgio Vasari (1511–74) was able to say of the Florentine painter Luca Signorelli (c.1440/50–1523), who rose to prominence in the years following Cosimo's death, that he "always lived more like a lord or an honored gentleman than a painter."

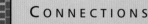

CONNECTIONS

The Influence of Classical Art

From the beginning, Renaissance scholars were influenced by the writings of ancient Greece and Rome. Yet apart from in architecture, where many Roman ruins remained to be studied, the artworks of the classical world were at first little known. Almost no paintings had survived, and the statues that had come down to the 15th century were mostly poor Roman copies of lost Greek originals.

The situation changed a little in High Renaissance times, when interest in the ancient world stimulated a wave of archaeological enquiry. Late in the 15th century a shepherd boy fell through a cleft in the Aventine Hills in Rome and found himself in a room full of painted figures. He had unknowingly discovered the cellars of the Golden House, a palace built by Emperor Nero in Rome in the 1st century C.E. Soon painters including Pinturicchio (c.1454–1513), Raphael (1483–1520), and Michelangelo (1475–1564) were having themselves lowered down on ropes to study the frescoes on its walls. Michelangelo was also strongly influenced by the 1st-century B.C.E. marble statue of *Laocoön and his Sons*, dug up nearby in 1506 and placed in the Belvedere Gardens at the Vatican.

AN EXTRA DIMENSION FOR PAINTING

The Florentine masters were especially sensitive about their standing, because Florence was the crucible of Renaissance art, inheriting an intellectual approach that could be traced all the way back to Giotto (c.1270–1337). In its studios and workshops, generations of scholars and artists applied the same sort of concentrated mental effort to understanding the rules of beauty that in the 20th century would go into

medical research or the quest to land humans on the Moon.

Their work was particularly significant for painting. What the High Renaissance pioneers were striving for was, literally, to add a whole new dimension to the art. The discovery of perspective had taken their works from a two-dimensional world of pattern and line into a third dimension of apparent depth. They now had to learn how to put the new space to work in the most effective way.

Early theorists like the architects Filippo Brunelleschi (1377–1446) and Leon Battista Alberti (1404–72) had sought the laws of perspective in mathematical theory, and their successors still retained something of their analytical approach; Leonardo da Vinci (1452–1519) for one showed an interest in the concept of the Golden Section (see box on page 35). Others worked more by trial and error to explore the new world of space composition, while always retaining a Florentine concern for rendering form and mass. By the end of the century the Byzantine tradition of flat silhouette had largely died out, as had the Byzantine Empire itself (its capital Constantinople had finally fallen to the Ottoman Turks in 1453 and been renamed Istanbul).

EXPLORING NEW THEMES

At the same time artists were also exploring new themes in their work. Recognizable landscapes came to replace the symbolic backdrops of Gothic paintings, in which an outline of jagged rocks had been enough to indicate that a painting was set in the mountains.

Besides getting more realistic, landscape also became a subject in its own right. The *Rape of Dejanira* by Antonio Pollaiuolo (c.1432–98) has been described as the first painting since Roman times in which the landscape was

Ideal City, ***attributed to the Sienese architect Francesco di Giorgio Martini (1439–1502). His*** **Treatise,** ***written in about 1480, is one of the milestones of architectural theory of the Italian Renaissance.***

Pisanello created a fashion for profile portraits, as in **Portrait of a Princess of the House of Este** *(1436–38).*

an integral part of the composition. In breaking new ground, the picture also showed the difficulties to be overcome—the artist had yet to solve the problem of how to integrate the foreground (seen from a ground-level viewpoint) with the aerial perspective of the distant scene. The end result was a picture that looked unbalanced.

Another breakthrough was the rediscovery of the nude body as a fitting subject for art. The inspiration came, like so much else in Renaissance times, from the classical heritage. In depicting the naked human form, painters and sculptors soon felt the need for a deeper understanding of how the body worked. Anatomical studies therefore joined experiments in perspective as part of the training of a new generation of artists.

Another feature of classical art that was rediscovered at this time was the portrait. Renaissance patrons' desire to immortalize themselves created a natural market for this branch of art, which had fallen into disuse in medieval times when art set out primarily to glorify God, not people. Antonio Pisanello (c.1394–?1455), a painter from Verona who worked in Venice and Rome, created a taste for portraits and portrait medals that showed the sitter in profile. Full-face images followed soon after.

PIERO DELLA FRANCESCA

While Florence was the creative hub of artistic progress in the 15th century, not all the innovators originally came from there. Piero della Francesca (c.1415–92) was born 60 miles (100 km) to the southwest in the small town of Borgo San Sepolcro. He learned much, however, from such Florentine masters as Uccello (c.1397–1475), Masaccio (1401–28/29), and Castagno (c.1418–57), and in time he became a model of the measured, theoretical approach to art associated with the city. In later life he published two Latin treatises on the theory of painting, basing his ideas on the laws of Euclidean geometry.

Piero's work also belonged in the Florentine tradition through its concern with form and mass and with mathematical proportion. What was new in his paintings was his taste for pale, soft colors and his use of effects of light to create a serene atmosphere even when depicting scenes of violent action.

Piero della Francesca's **The Resurrection of Christ** *(1464–65) is a fresco he painted for his home city, Borgo San Sepolcro.*

 See also: The Pre- and Early Renaissance **8–27**

Mantegna used dramatic foreshortening effects in his ceiling fresco for the Camera Picta at the Palazzo Ducale, Mantua (1465–74).

The result was a timeless style that conveys an impression of impassivity and stillness. A work such as *The Dream of Constantine* (c.1466) also illustrates his taste for solving problems of perspective, visible in the figure of the plunging angel come to reveal to the sleeping Roman emperor the vision of the True Cross.

MANTEGNA AND THE PADUA SCHOOL

Andrea Mantegna (c.1431–1506) was another non-Florentine who worked in a tradition deeply marked by the city's art. He came from Padua in northern Italy, but was influenced by the sculptor

Donatello (c.1386–1466), who moved there from Florence in 1443. Drawing also on the perspective studies of such artists as Uccello, Mantegna developed a hard, monumental style, often featuring foreshortening effects. Venerating ancient Rome, he set out to create an idealized image of antiquity. His paintings are populated by stately figures set against rocky backdrops, giving them great dignity. Yet, as critics have pointed out, he sometimes seems to be painting statues rather than real people.

Mantegna's style was taken up by his successors in Padua and by painters in nearby Ferrara, notably Cosimo Tura (c.1430–95). Tura and his followers exaggerated Mantegna's hard sculptural style into a stony expressionism that was at the opposite extreme of Renaissance art from the soft manner of the Umbrian School (see box on page 48–49).

TOOLS AND TECHNIQUES

The Golden Section

Throughout the 15th century Florentine artists and theorists sought to find a mathematical basis for beauty, believing it to lie in what the architect Leon Battista Alberti (1404–72) called "the harmonious combination of different parts in a consistent whole." The culmination of the search for perfect proportion, whether in buildings, paintings, or even human features, came in a work called *De divina proportione* (Concerning Divine Proportion), written at the end of the 14th century by a monk and mathematician, Fra Luca di Pacioli (c.1445–c.1514). Pacioli was a fellow townsman of the painter Piero della Francesca (c.1415–92), and the work is thought to have reflected Piero's own ideas.

The Golden Section itself, defined as the division of a line so that the shorter part is to the longer as the longer is to the whole, was put to use by many painters, sculptors, and architects. Leonardo da Vinci (1452–1519) was a friend of Pacioli's, and the proportional drawings he made in his sketchbooks in the 1490s show that he was working along similar lines of enquiry.

THE FLORENTINE CRUCIBLE

It was in Florence itself that the main advances continued to be made. Writing in the mid-16th century, Vasari sought to explain the reasons for its primacy, settling on three separate factors. The first was the city's critical frame of mind for, in his words, "the air of Florence breeds naturally free spirits not generally content with mediocre work." The second was a lack of natural resources in the surrounding lands that forced the citizens to work hard and look to their own talents to earn a living. Thirdly, he picked out the "lust for glory and honor" that in his view distinguished Florentines of every profession.

In the generation after Donatello, one aspect of the Florentine genius continued to express itself in sculpture. The great man's legacy was maintained by such individuals as Bertoldo di Giovanni (c.1420–91), a pupil of Donatello's who himself became the master of the great painter and sculptor Michelangelo (1475–1564). Another of Bertoldo's pupils was Andrea Sansovino (c.1467/70–1529), a graceful craftsman who worked in Portugal and Rome as well as in Florence.

THE DELLA ROBBIA FAMILY

A separate tradition developed around the workshop of Luca della Robbia (c.1399–1482), a master who applied the vitrified glazes used by potters to terra-cotta sculptures, making them exceptionally durable and suitable for decorating even the outsides of buildings. According to Vasari, the original attraction of the technique for della Robbia was that clay was quicker to work than marble or bronze, so enabling him to boost his income. Another advantage was that the glazes could preserve colors, allowing him to produce hundreds of low-relief sculptures, often round or semicircular in form, set against Wedgwood-blue backgrounds, which brightened the interiors and exteriors of churches and palaces. The works proved so popular that they became the basis of a flourishing family business that lasted well into the 16th century.

Bertoldo di Giovanni's most famous bronze sculpture,* Bellerophon and Pegasus *(c.1480), represents the Greek hero Bellerophon (symbolizing courage) attempting to tame Pegasus (symbolizing immortality).

ANDREA DEL VERROCCHIO

The greatest of Donatello's successors, however, was Andrea del Verrocchio (c.1435–88). Verrocchio was a true Renaissance man who won fame not just as a sculptor but also as a painter and goldsmith and as the man in whose workshop Leonardo da Vinci first learned his art. Having started his career working in precious metals, he was won over to sculpture while working in Rome by the discovery of some newly excavated ancient Roman statues. Subsequently, he turned his hand to painting but reportedly gave it up for good when he realized he could never match the talent of his pupil Leonardo.

Verrocchio is best remembered for his sculpture, including a bronze bust of his patron Lorenzo de' Medici, or Lorenzo the Magnificent (1449–92), that is the best-known surviving likeness of the

 See also: The Late Renaissance and Mannerism 70–89

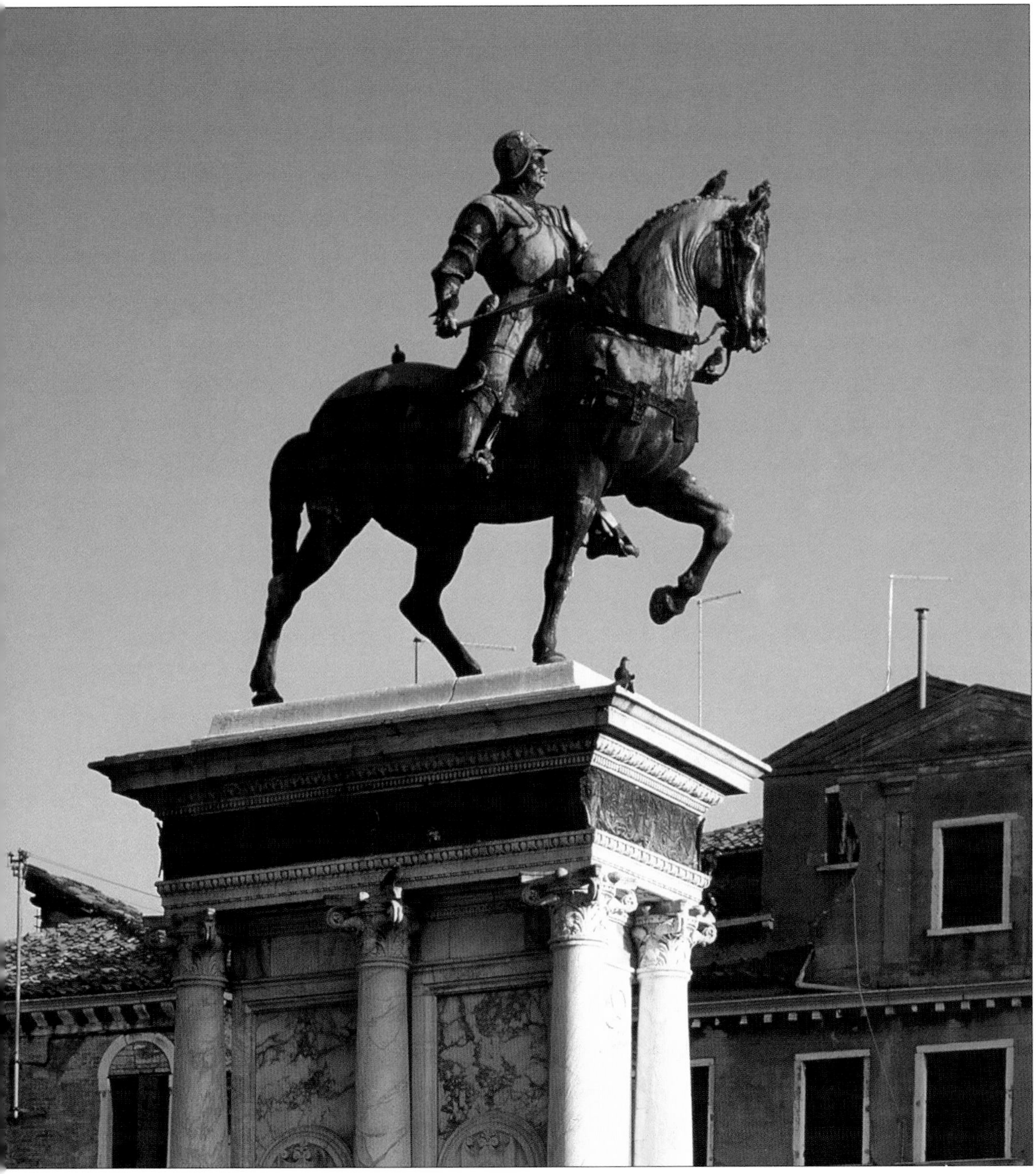

The sculptor Verrocchio was commissioned to create a monument to the mercenary soldier Bartolomeo Colleoni of Bergamo, who died in 1475. The resulting statue in Venice's Square of Saints John and Paul was unfinished at the time of Verrocchio's death in 1488, but was unveiled posthumously in 1496.

ruler. Equally fine is the horseback statue of Bartolomeo Colleoni (1400–75) that still stands in a square in Venice. Colleoni was the very model of the freelance mercenary leaders, or *condottieri*, who rose to prominence in the countless small wars of 15th-century Italy. Verrocchio captures the pride and vigor of a man who has made himself master of all he surveys.

THE FLORENTINE PAINTERS

A distinctive feature of Renaissance Italy was the number of multitalented artists it produced. Verrocchio's contemporary Antonio Pollaiuolo also put his hand to many forms of art, but in his case left his major mark on painting. His particular interest lay in the portrayal of violent

In **An Old Man and a Boy** *(c.1485) Ghirlandaio realistically portrays the old man's rugged features, while at the same time conveying the gentle relationship between grandfather and grandson.*

action, taking the solid, three-dimensional bodies mastered by Masaccio and showing them in motion under stress. Antonio and his younger brother Piero (c.1441–c.96) were among the first artists to dissect bodies in order to understand how they worked. One of Antonio's best-known works is an engraving known as the *Battle of the Nudes*, showing naked warriors locked in combat (now in the Louvre Museum, Paris).

Antonio Pollaiuolo's concern with form and mass was a typically Florentine trait, described by the theorist Leon Battista Alberti as "a product of the mind" in contrast to surface realism, which was merely "borrowed from nature."

His contemporary Domenico Ghirlandaio (c.1449–94) shared his approach. The finest fresco painter of his generation, Ghirlandaio also produced some charming paintings in tempera—paints made by mixing pigments with egg yolk diluted with water—including a well-known portrait of a bulbous-nosed old man with a boy. Like the sculptor Bertoldo, he had the young Michelangelo as his apprentice for a while.

A separate tradition in Florentine painting developed through a colorful character named Fra Filippo Lippi (c.1406–69), who was orphaned and placed in a Carmelite monastery in his youth. Although he never renounced his monastic vows, he does not seem to have had a religious bent: At one stage he ran away with a novice from a nunnery where he had been commissioned to do a painting. The girl subsequently gave birth to a son, Filippino Lippi (c.1457–1504), who in his turn became a famous painter.

While strongly influenced by the Florentine masters of form, particularly Masaccio, Lippi also showed an interest in narrative painting and was perhaps the finest colorist of his generation. He passed on these attributes to his pupil Sandro Botticelli (c.1445–1510), who in later life would serve as the master of Filippino Lippi.

Sandro Botticelli

Botticelli was one of the most exquisite masters of line in all art and came to outdo even Filippo Lippi as a colorist. Yet his works, which are among the supreme achievements of the High Renaissance, remain outside the main tradition of Florentine painting, their grace and delicacy harking back instead to the earlier tradition of Sienese art (see box on page 15).

In his youth Botticelli was known as a practical joker, but in his 50s he went through a religious crisis, becoming a follower of the puritan monk Savonarola (1452–98) (see box on page 40). He

MASTERPIECE

Botticelli's Primavera

Sandro Botticelli's *Primavera* (Spring), shown below, hangs in the Uffizi Gallery in Florence. It was painted in about 1482 for Lorenzo di Pierfrancesco de' Medici, a cousin of Lorenzo the Magnificent (1449–92). It was apparently planned as a companion piece for another, equally famous work, *The Birth of Venus* (c.1484).

In both works Venus, the Roman goddess of love, is the central figure. In *Primavera* she appears in a wooded orange grove. To her right are the Three Graces, goddesses of beauty and fertility. Turning away from them is Mercury, messenger of the Roman gods, identified by winged sandals and wooden wand. On Venus's left are Primavera herself, personifying the springtime, flanked by Flora, goddess of spring, who wears a diaphanous gown and is clutched in the rough embrace of her husband, the wind god Zephyr.

Botticelli found the painting's theme in poems by the Neo-Platonist Politian (1454–94)—like the painter himself, he was a member of the Medici inner circle. Art historians interpret the work as an allegory: Venus represents spiritual love, Zephyr physical lust, and Mercury human reason, which can dispel clouds of error but turns its back on the spiritual love worshiped by the Neo-Platonists.

abandoned painting entirely in his last years, living instead on the charity of his friends and former patrons.

The eccentric Piero di Cosimo (c.1461–?1521) was another Florentine painter. In his youth Piero gained favor by designing carnival floats, including a macabre *Triumph of Death* that caused a huge sensation. Throughout his life he continued to be fascinated by the bizarre and the grotesque, and in old age he became a recluse. Vasari described how he would stare at stained walls or clouds in the sky and see in them panoramic battle scenes or fantastic cityscapes. His fanciful vision lives on in paintings such as *The Forest Fire* (c.1505) and *The Discovery of Honey* (c.1505–10).

CONNECTIONS

The Bonfire of the Vanities

The Renaissance for the most part celebrated worldly magnificence, but the mood sometimes swung back toward medieval piety and the fear of God's wrath. This was never more the case than in Florence between 1495 and 1498, when the city came under the domination of the puritan monk Savonarola (1452–98). In 1497, as part of his campaign against worldly vanities, Savonarola organized a huge public burning of luxury goods and art objects, ranging from fine dresses and cosmetics to books and paintings that he considered immoral. Among the latter were some paintings on mythological themes by Botticelli (c.1445–1510), which the artist placed on the pyre himself in a fit of remorse. A year later, popular opinion swung again, this time against the preacher. Accused of religious error, Savonarola was himself burned at the stake in the very square where the artworks had been torched.

LEONARDO DA VINCI

The greatest of all the Florentine masters was Leonardo da Vinci, who was recognized in his own lifetime as a unique and irreplaceable genius. The son of a lawyer, he was born in 1452 in the village of Vinci outside Florence. Recognizing the boy's talent for drawing, his father sent him to work at the age of 17 as an apprentice in Verrocchio's workshop, where he remained for nine years. Thereafter he lived a wandering life, moving between Milan, Florence, and Rome until Francis I of France (1494–1547) persuaded him to move to his palace of Amboise in the Loire region. Leonardo spent the last three years of his life there, dying in 1519.

Painting was only one aspect of Leonardo's talent. He showed an equal interest in engineering projects, working as a military engineer and once even writing to the Ottoman sultan offering to bridge the inlet in Istanbul known as the Golden Horn. He had a scientist's interest in botany, geology, and anatomy. He once wrote to a friend to describe how he had just dissected 10 bodies: "You might be put off," he noted, "by the fear of living

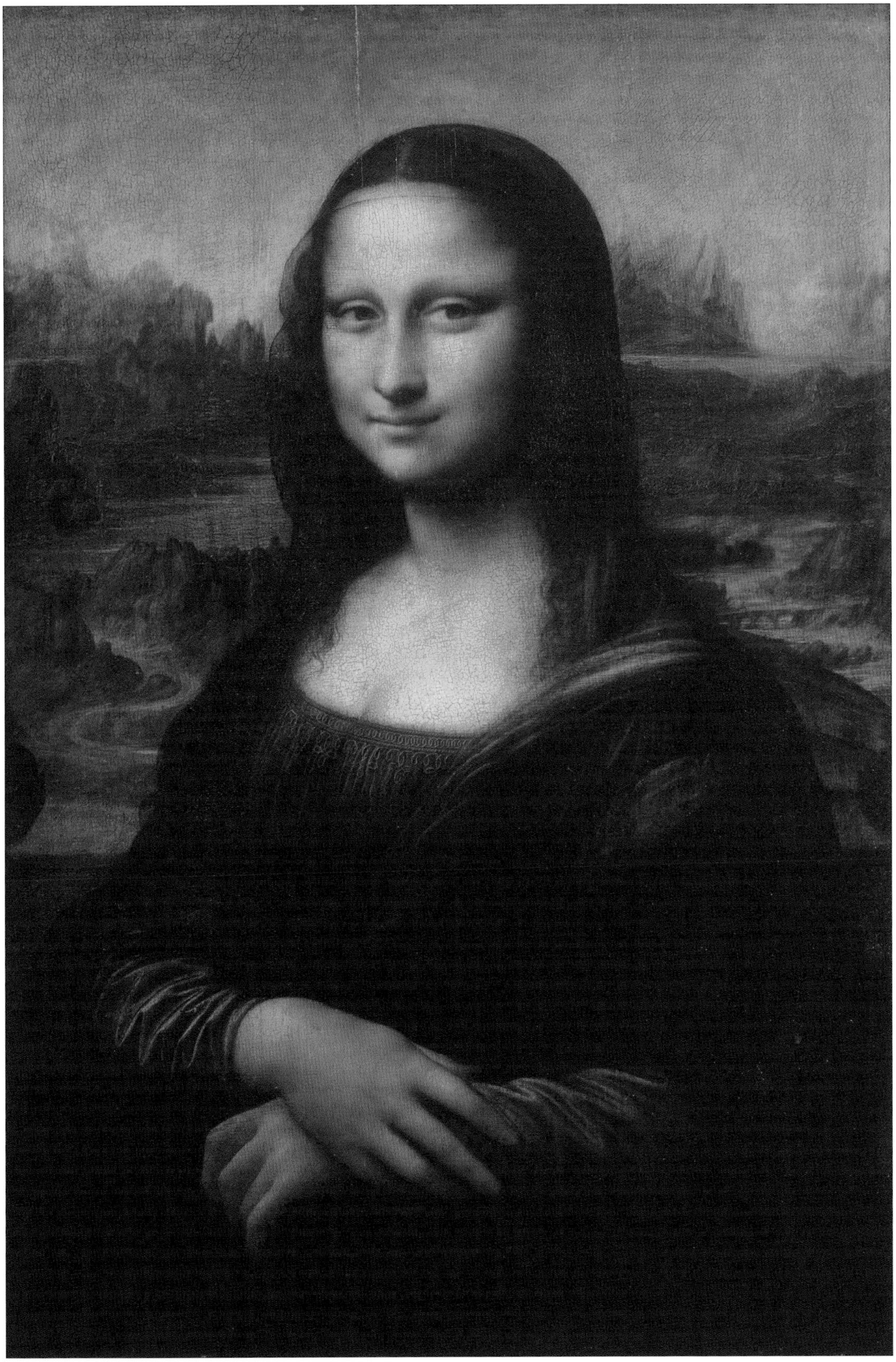

Mona Lisa *(c.1503–06) by Leonardo da Vinci. The sitter's enigmatic smile has fascinated people for centuries. In the portrait Leonardo used* sfumato*—the blending of colors to create a misty effect. The* Mona Lisa *owes its timeless appeal to our feeling that we are engaging with a real person who has an inner vitality that is nonetheless elusive.*

through the night hours in the company of these corpses, quartered and flayed and horrible to behold."

He was an inventor, sketching farsighted plans for submarines and helicopters, even a factory for mass-producing pins. Some of his notions were more light-hearted—reportedly he once stuck wings on an odd-shaped lizard to make it look like a miniature dragon, and he also devised a way of blowing up cleaned pig's intestines with a bellows so that they filled an entire room.

Leonardo also made major advances in painting. He developed the technique known as *sfumato* ("shaded") to soften the transition between different patches of color, and also devised his own form of aerial perspective to convey distant landscapes.

His caring personality, which in life led him sometimes to buy caged birds simply to set them free, found its way into his art, giving much of his work a quality that his contemporaries called *dolcezza* (sweetness).

Yet he could also produce works of intense violence—deluges, whirlwinds, and battle scenes. His one great problem was impatience: His roving mind was so active that he rarely bothered to finish his works. Only a handful of completed paintings have survived, although notebooks containing thousands of sketches have been found, together with explanatory notes. Intriguingly, he chose to write his notes backward, so observers have to hold them up to a mirror to read them.

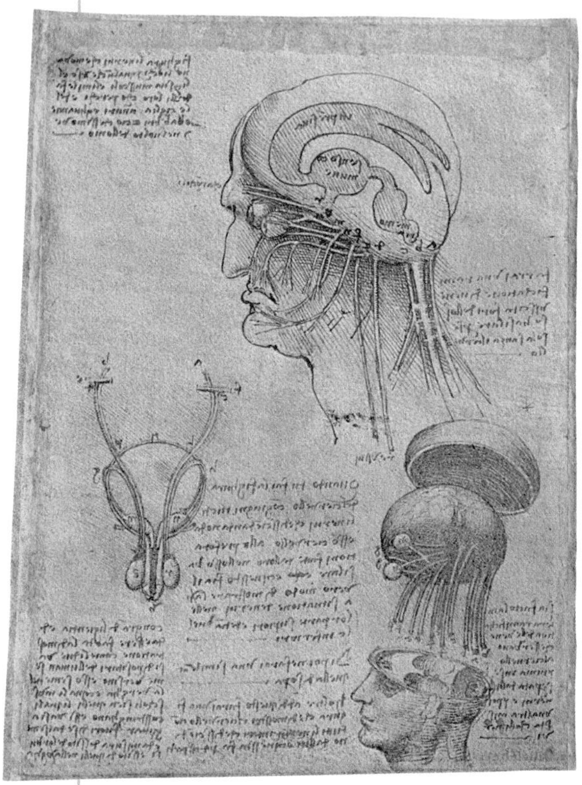

In attempts to discover how the human body and mind worked, Leonardo made anatomical sketches and recorded his ideas in notebooks using "mirror" writing. These drawings of the brain, ventricles, and cerebral nerves were made in about 1500.

THE VENETIAN SCHOOL

By Leonardo's day another school had arisen to challenge the preeminence of the Florentines. The port city of Venice had produced fine painters in earlier generations, among them Gentile da Fabriano (c.1385–1427), who worked in the International Gothic style, and Carlo Crivelli (c.1430–1494), who was responsible for ornate, richly textured works such as the *Annunciation* (1486).

It was only in the latter part of the 15th century that a specifically Venetian style of art developed—largely through the influence of one family, the Bellinis, who produced a dynasty of talented painters. The greatest of them was Giovanni Bellini (1430–1516), a hugely influential master whose work exemplified the main qualities for which Venetian painting would become famous: the handling of color and light.

If Florentine painting was intellectual in its inspiration, the Venetian

Masterpiece

Leonardo's Virgin and Child with Saint Anne

The *Virgin and Child with Saint Anne* (c.1508) by Leonardo da Vinci, seen right, shows three generations of the holy family. The Virgin Mary leans forward to protect the infant Jesus, seen playing with a lamb, while Mary's mother, Saint Anne, looks on fondly. The lamb is an image of innocence and sacrifice, symbolizing Christ's future passion and crucifixion. Mary's role is that of the loving mother, while Saint Anne's tender detachment may be an allegory of the Church, which knows the inevitability of Jesus' fate.

The theme fascinated Leonardo over many years. He produced a full-sized preparatory drawing as early as 1498. The painting itself, still not completely finished, is known to have been in his possession shortly before his death.

The stony foreground is carefully worked, suggesting Leonardo's interest in geology, but the background of misty mountains is sketched only vaguely. The evidence of preliminary versions suggests Leonardo worked hard on the arrangement of the figures, striving to combine naturalness with a basically pyramidal composition that was to prove hugely influential, serving as a model for later canvases by such artists as Andrea del Sarto (1486–1530) and Raphael (1483–1520). The painting illustrates Leonardo's *sfumato* technique, its misty effect softening tones and indicating distance. But the work's enduring popularity derives from its iconic portrayal of maternal love, being bathed in an emotional warmth that radiates across the centuries.

style was sensuous. The city's wealthy ruling class enjoyed a life of ease and refinement, and they cherished an art that appealed to the emotions more than the rational mind. Maybe too the effect of the radiant Adriatic sun, filtered through the watery atmosphere of the city's canals and lagoons, played its part in mellowing painters' palettes. For whatever reasons, the best Venetian paintings seem bathed in a warm glow that marks them out from those of any other school.

BELLINI AND HIS FOLLOWERS

Bellini himself was a particularly versatile talent whose works ranged from the spareness of *Saint Francis in the Desert* (c.1480–85) to the pagan richness of such late works as *The Feast of the Gods* (c.1514),

Bellini's* The Feast of the Gods *(c.1514) was one of the few paintings the artist executed on canvas rather than wooden panels. It illustrates a story from Ovid featuring Roman gods and goddesses.

 See also: The Late Renaissance and Mannerism **70–89**

prefiguring the style of (and possibly finished by) his onetime pupil Titian (c.1485–1576). What links all his work is a rendering of atmosphere, linked with strong drawing and a total mastery of perspective that makes him almost unsurpassed in the art of depicting figures in a landscape.

Many of the next generation of Venetian artists actively worked with Bellini or, like Cima da Conegliano (c.1459/60–1517/18), who painted calm, richly colored religious works, came under his influence. This was also the case with Vittore Carpaccio (c.1460–1525/6), the painter of a famous *Saint George and the Dragon* (1504–07) and of a beautiful *Sacra Conversazione* (c.1500).

THE INFLUENCE OF GIORGIONE

One of the greatest Venetian artists, Giorgione (c.1477–1510), was once Bellini's pupil. In his short life Giorgione produced relatively little. Only about half a dozen works survive that are indisputably by him, yet they include masterpieces that helped change the course of painting. Though he also painted large frescoes that are now lost, Giorgione set a fashion for small oil paintings destined for the homes of private collectors. Some were portraits, at which he excelled. Others belonged to a new kind of work whose subject matter was consciously poetic and private, not drawn from the Bible or classical mythology. The finest is probably *The Tempest* (c.1508). In the foreground a young man leans on a staff, watching a naked woman breastfeeding an infant on the opposite bank of a stream; in the background a storm breaks over a town.

The picture possibly illustrates an incident from a book or a legend but, if that is the case, scholars have never managed to identify it. The real subject of the painting is its extraordinary light—the electric, highly charged atmosphere that precedes a summer storm.

The Tempest *(c.1508) is typical of Giorgione's style: It is a small-scale work with an elusive and mysterious subject.*

RAPHAEL

After Giorgione's death from the plague in 1510, painting became a matter of personal vision to a greater extent than ever before. Yet it never lost its other, civic function, namely of decorating large public spaces.

The last great genius of the High Renaissance years combined both these roles in a life that was barely longer than that of Giorgione. Raffaelo Sanzio, known to posterity as Raphael (1483–1520), died of a fever on his 37th birthday, by which time he had already established himself—along with Leonardo and Michelangelo—as one of the supreme masters of Italian painting. High Renaissance art can be said to have reached its full flowering with his arrival in Rome in 1508 and to have passed away with his death 12 years later.

Raphael's artistic background lay in the tranquil beauties of the Umbrian School (see box on page 48). He came from its artistic capital, Urbino, where he trained in the workshop of its greatest master, Perugino (c.1450–1523), whose work strongly influenced his own early paintings. Yet the young man was to prove chameleonlike in his ability to absorb new influences. In Florence between 1505 and 1508, he came across the work of Leonardo, rapidly mastering his technique of *sfumato*. Raphael was in Rome when the Sistine Chapel ceiling was revealed, and he learned from Michelangelo's masterpiece how to bring more action into his own large compositions.

The fact was that Raphael married a stupendous natural talent with a passion for hard work and an infinite capacity to learn. He had a phenomenal visual imagination—so much so that the images he created of the Madonna and of great figures from classical mythology have shaped people's images of them to the present day.

He was also possibly the greatest master of pictorial composition in the history of art, with a unique ability to group figures in seemingly spontaneous

Raphael's many depictions of the Madonna and Child, including **Madonna del Granduca** *(c.1505), shown left, were created during his time in Florence, where he was inspired by Leonardo and Michelangelo.*

School of Athens *(c.1510–12) is one of the frescoes created by Raphael for apartments in the Vatican. It celebrates the great masters of classical philosophy and includes in the center the figures of Plato (pointing up) and Aristotle (gesturing down, toward the world of earthly experience).*

 See also: The Late Renaissance and Mannerism **70–89**

SCHOOLS AND MOVEMENTS

Neo-Platonism

When the early Renaissance rediscovered classical learning its thinking was dominated by the Greek philosopher Aristotle (382–322 B.C.E.). Aristotle had promoted an ordered mindset and believed people should use reason and the evidence of their senses to understand the world around them. By High Renaissance times some scholars found this line of thought arid, and turned instead to another ancient Greek thinker, Plato (c.427–c.347 B.C.E.). These Neo-Platonists stressed the importance of abstract ideas, particularly the concept of beauty, which they treated as an almost religious ideal that could bring people closer to God. The movement was patronized by the Medici rulers of Florence and had a marked effect on art, encouraging painters to abandon surface realism in favor of a quest for perfect harmony. Sandro Botticelli (c.1445–1510) was particularly influenced by Neo-Platonist ideas, which left their mark on such masterpieces as *The Birth of Venus* (c.1484).

but infinitely harmonious ways. The feeling of space that he brought to some of his works transports the viewer to a happier, more harmonious universe.

A NEW PROBLEM FOR ART

In the last years of his short life Raphael became something of a victim of his own success. A popular figure, he was inundated with more commissions than he could easily handle. The problem grew worse after 1514, when he took on the job of principal architect to St. Peter's Basilica in Rome.

He had a large workshop of well-trained apprentices and increasingly he entrusted them with filling in the detail of his works, confining his own attentions to the grand design. Yet the quality remained high, and he continued to please his patrons. By the time of his death there was even talk of his being made a cardinal as a reward for his years of service to the Church.

In his work Raphael gathered all the strands that Italian painters had been struggling to bring together since Giotto's day. The mastery of three-dimensional space was at last complete, and artists could in future seek not just to rival but to surpass nature. Now a new problem arose to trouble succeeding generations: What could they paint now that would not simply seem like an inferior copy of Leonardo or Raphael?

The Umbrian School

A distinguishing feature of the Italian Renaissance was the development of distinctive schools of painting in provincial towns away from the main artistic centers of Rome, Florence, and Siena. One of the most important flourished in the Umbria region of central Italy at Urbino near the regional capital of Perugia. The Umbrian School inherited the mantle of Sienese painting, producing gentle refined works marked by fresh colors and—in its case—beautiful landscape backgrounds.

The impetus for the school's development seems to have come from Siena and from artists such as Gentile da Fabriano (c.1385–1427), the chief Italian exponent of the International Gothic manner. Its own style reached maturity in the late 15th century in the work of two contemporaries and colleagues, Pinturicchio (c.1454–1513) and Pietro Perugino (c.1450–1523).

Pinturicchio's tranquilly poetic works, marked by skilled portraiture and a flair for narrative detail, made him popular with patrons, the more so because he worked quickly to commission. Although his later works became formulaic, his earlier paintings, according to the critic Bernard Berenson (1865–1959), "are among the most faithful representations of refined splendor and elegance of living."

Perugino studied in Florence in the same workshop as Leonardo da Vinci (1452–1519), and he developed a calm, serene style that greatly influenced Raphael (1483–1520), who was his pupil for four years. Sadly, he lived long enough to go out of fashion; in his last years his gentle manner was swept away by the passionate violence of Michelangelo (1475–1564).

Perugino's* Lamentation Over the Dead Christ *(1495) is one of many religious pictures, created for churches, that helped the viewer to imagine scenes from the Bible. Here the treatment of the landscape in particular, using fresh rather than vivid colors, is typical of the Umbrian School.

 See also: The Pre- and Early Renaissance **8–27**

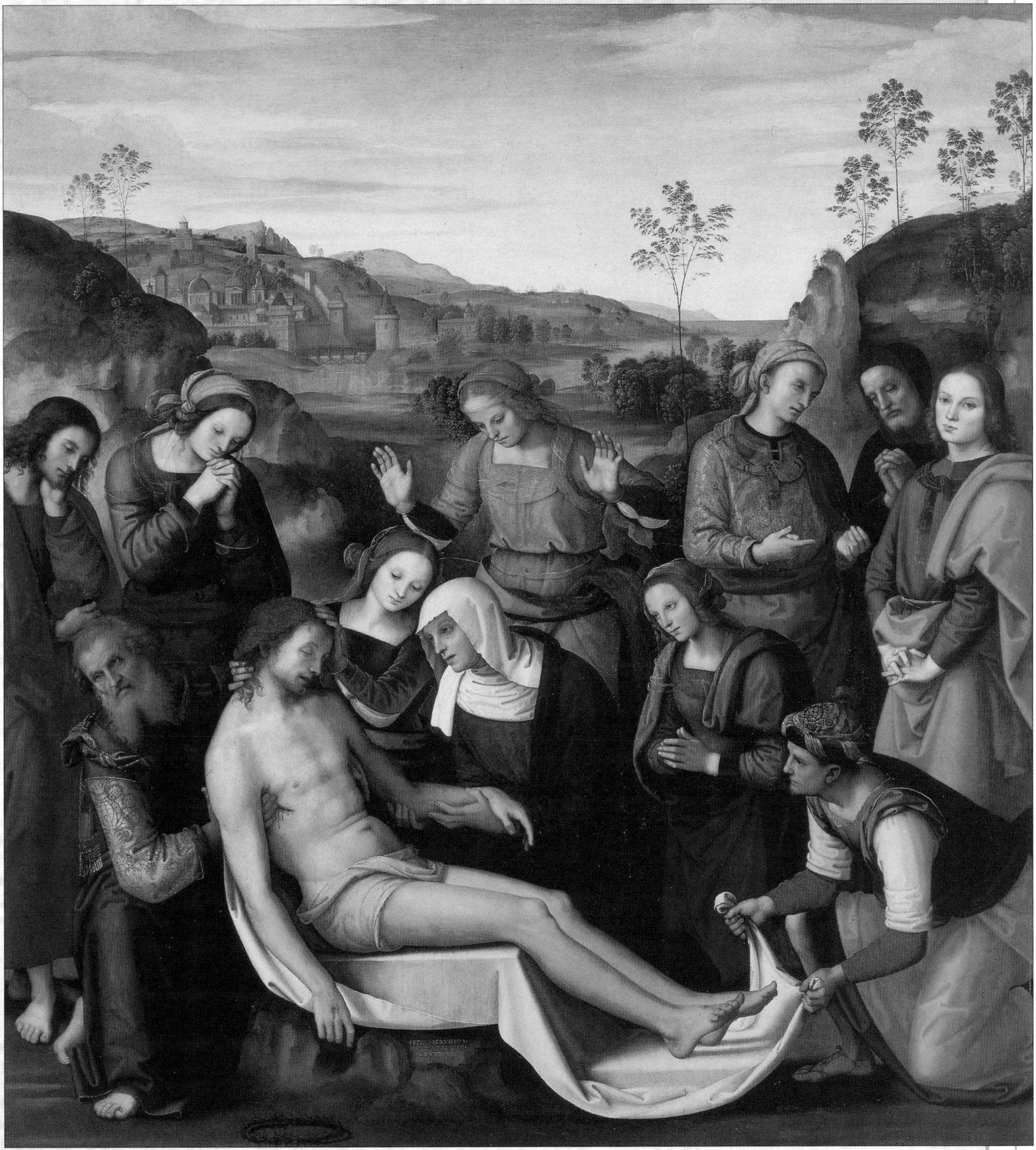

c.1450–1525

The Northern Renaissance

The Renaissance in northern Europe produced great masters such as Holbein, Bosch, Grünewald, van Eyck, and Dürer. During this period art in the north had a character that was distinct from that of Italy. While the styles of individual artists varied, one characteristic they shared was the meticulous rendering of detail. They were also generally less influenced than their Italian counterparts by the classical Greek and Roman ideal in their representation of figures.

While the High Renaissance was underway in Italy, the lands to the north were also experiencing an artistic flowering. For most people the 14th century had been disastrous, marked by war and plague—specifically the Black Death, a pandemic thought to have killed one-third of Europe's population. But by the 15th century things were on the mend. The number of citizens was rising, and they were increasingly employed in new ways. The feudal system, under which most people had worked on the land, was breaking up, and more and more people were flocking to the towns.

Across Europe cities were booming. In Flanders, Antwerp more than doubled its population to about 50,000 in the second half of the 15th century, then doubled it again by 1560. In Germany Augsburg became the headquarters of the Fugger banking dynasty, whose intercontinental connections came to rival those of the Italian Medici family. In England, London developed as a thriving business center, while in Spain and Portugal, Seville and Lisbon grew rich from trading contacts with new lands discovered by ocean explorers.

AN INTELLECTUAL REVIVAL

With the new wealth came new ideas. Students who, early in the 15th century, would have had to go to Italy to acquire a

 See also: The Pre- and Early Renaissance **8–27**; The High Renaissance in Italy **28–49**

humanist education were soon able to do so at home. By the early 16th century the northern lands were producing their own intellectual heavyweights such as Erasmus (1466–1536) in the Netherlands and England's Sir Thomas More (1478–1535), author of the original alternative-world novel *Utopia*. Their ideas were disseminated by movable-type printing, pioneered in about 1450 by Johannes Gutenberg. The new technology spread rapidly, and by 1500 there were 6 million printed books in circulation.

There were significant differences between the intellectual climates in Italy and the north. Alongside the humanist tradition, a deep vein of spirituality found expression in a flood of mystical writings—among them the sermons of the 14th-century German theologian Meister Eckhart (c.1260–1327/8) and *The Imitation of Christ* by Thomas à Kempis (1380–1471). The movement known as the *Devotio Moderna* (Modern Devotion) encouraged a more individual attitude towards religious belief and a life of simple devotion. It gave rise to new lay religious societies such as the Brethren of the Common Life and to the founding of Dominican monasteries.

The Last Supper *(1464–67) by Dierec Bouts was a commission for the Church of St. Peter in Leuven, where it still forms the central part of the altarpiece.*

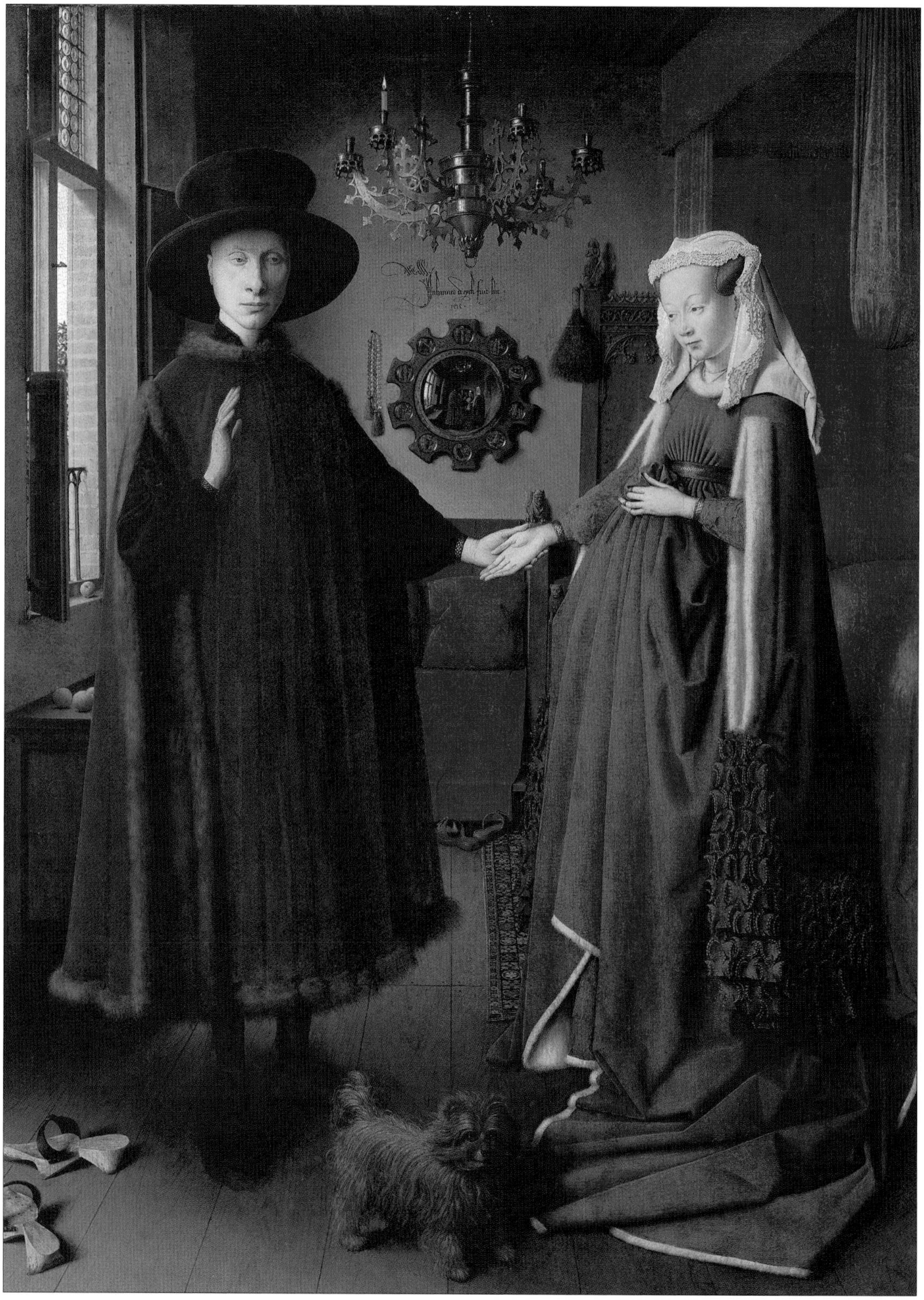

Portrait of Giovanni Arnolfini and His Wife *(also known as* **The Arnolfini Wedding***), 1434. In this painting van Eyck produced an image of outstanding clarity and realism—yet for all its naturalness, the scene is full of signs and symbols. For example, the dog is thought to represent fidelity and the discarded shoes may signify respect for the marriage ceremony.*

Religious faith permeated northern painting, from the gentle piety of such artists as Dierec Bouts (c.1420–75) and Hans Memlinc (c.1430/40–94) to the passionate expressionism of Matthias Grünewald (c.1475/80–1528) or the unknown individual who painted the Villeneuve-lès-Avignon *Pietà* (c.1455).

 See also: The High Renaissance in Italy **28–49**

ART ACROSS BORDERS

Northern painters learned much from their Italian counterparts in other respects at this time. One means of communication was through the merchants and bankers, who were wealthy enough to serve as valued patrons and also operated on a continental scale. One of the seminal works of Jan van Eyck (c.1390–1441), *Portrait of Giovanni Arnolfini and His Wife* (1434), was of an Italian banker working in Bruges in the Netherlands. The Portinari Altarpiece, a hugely influential work by the Flemish artist Hugo van der Goes (c.1440–82), was commissioned by a Medici representative in Bruges to decorate a church in Florence.

There were dangers in transporting works of art from one country to another, as was shown when a Hans Memlinc altarpiece shipped from Flanders to the Mediterranean ended up in the Baltic port of Gdansk, having been seized by pirates along the way. Yet the overall effect was overwhelmingly positive.

If artworks traveled, so did artists. The French painter Jean Fouquet (1420–79) is thought to have visited Rome as early as the 1440s, and the Flemish master Rogier van der Weyden (c.1399–1464) was probably there shortly afterward. Albrecht Dürer (see pages 68 to 69) made two well-documented visits—as a young man in 1494 and as an established master in 1506, when the great Giovanni Bellini (1430–1516), among others, sought to buy his works.

It was particularly in the fields of perspective and three-dimensional composition that artists in the north learned from their Italian counterparts. Yet they also brought much of their own to the exchange. Collectively, their works were distinguished by a taste for realism and a careful attention to sometimes homely detail.

CONNECTIONS

Naples and the Netherlands

In Renaissance times unlikely ties between corners of the continent were created by Europe's ruling families, including one between southern Italy and the Netherlands. The Austrian Hapsburg Dynasty acquired the Netherlands in 1477 when Maximilian I (1459–1519) married the heiress of the previous rulers, the dukes of Burgundy. Maximilian's son Philip (1478–1506) subsequently married the heiress to the Spanish throne. Spain's rulers had long-held claims to the kingdom of Naples in the south of Italy, which they finally won by force in 1504. The various possessions eventually came together in the hands of the Holy Roman Emperor Charles V (1500–58), who ruled Spain, Naples, and the Netherlands as well as the imperial lands in Germany.

Artistically, the result was to forge links between artists in distant lands. The main conduit for Flemish influence in Italy was Antonello da Messina (c.1430–79), an artist born in Sicily. Antonello first came across Flemish art as an apprentice in Naples. He later worked in Venice, introducing techniques pioneered by the van Eycks and Rogier van der Weyden (c.1399–1464) to the masters of the Venetian School, notably Giovanni Bellini.

Madonna and Child *by Rogier van der Weyden (c.1450–60). The devotion to detail and subtle hues that characterize van der Weyden's work create a subdued, thoughtful mood.*

On the surface, they seemed less concerned with conventional notions of beauty: For example, the nudes painted by Flemish and German painters of the time appear relatively clumsy and unshapely when placed beside the works of Raphael (1483–1520) or Titian (c.1485–1576). Yet they showed an extraordinary feeling for the natural world and an ability to combine large vistas with precise detail.

THE ART OF FLANDERS

The region that came closest to challenging Italy's pride of place in the High Renaissance years was the Netherlands, and particularly the southern region known as Flanders. Politically the Netherlands was ruled by the dukes of Burgundy until 1477, when it passed through marriage to the Hapsburg rulers of Austria and then to Spain.

Significantly, Flanders was the region of northern Europe that economically and socially came closest to northern Italy. It too was heavily urbanized: Bruges, Ghent, Brussels, and Antwerp took the place there of Siena, Florence, Rome, and Venice. Wool merchants were the Flemish equivalent of the bankers of northern Italy, and they too proved happy to patronize the arts.

The Flemish tradition had been established early in the 15th century by the van Eyck brothers, who first provided the formula for northern realism. They also introduced the note of sober grace that was to be a continuing feature of Netherlandish painting. Rogier van der Weyden added a wider expressive range and a more open portrayal of emotion. On these foundations the Flemish artists of the later 15th century constructed one of the great schools of world art.

The outstanding characteristic of Flemish art was its close observation of the physical world. This would come to irritate Michelangelo (1475–1564) who, as a true Florentine, thought that painting should incorporate a big idea. "They paint in Flanders only to deceive the external eye ..." he wrote. "Their painting is of stuffs, bricks and mortar, the grass of the fields, the shadows of trees, and bridges and rivers, which they call landscapes… ." This criticism fails to take into account, however, the remarkable feeling for textures and surfaces that was one of the strengths of these Flemish painters, along with the ability to capture them on canvas in precise brushstrokes.

One of the most influential figures of the mid-15th century was Dierec Bouts.

Born in Haarlem, he ended his career as city painter for the town of Leuven, where he died, leaving two sons to carry on the family tradition. Bouts learned from Rogier van der Weyden, whose work he probably studied in Brussels.

In comparison with Rogier's, the figures in his paintings are stiff and unemotional, and their poses can seem ungainly. Yet works such as *The Way to Paradise* (1450) are redeemed by fine color, rich textures, beautiful landscape backgrounds, and above all a delicate handling of light. Bouts's treatment of religious subjects was typically Flemish—he generally chose to show them in everyday settings, while the figures portrayed often wear contemporary dress. His work was widely admired and would influence later artists, particularly in Germany.

BRUGES—ARTISTIC CENTER

The Eyckian heritage was particularly cherished in Bruges, where Jan van Eyck had spent his final years. His closest pupil was Petrus Christus (c.1410–75/6), who may have finished van Eyck's final work, *Madonna and Child with Saints* (c.1441), and probably took over his workshop. Petrus continued to paint in his master's style, although the forms in his paintings are slightly smoother and more rounded. His work found its way to Italy, where it influenced Antonello da Messina (c.1430–79), van Eyck's chief Italian disciple.

By the middle of the 15th century Bruges was becoming a magnet for painters (see box on page 56) and began to attract artists even from outside the Netherlands. One such was Hans

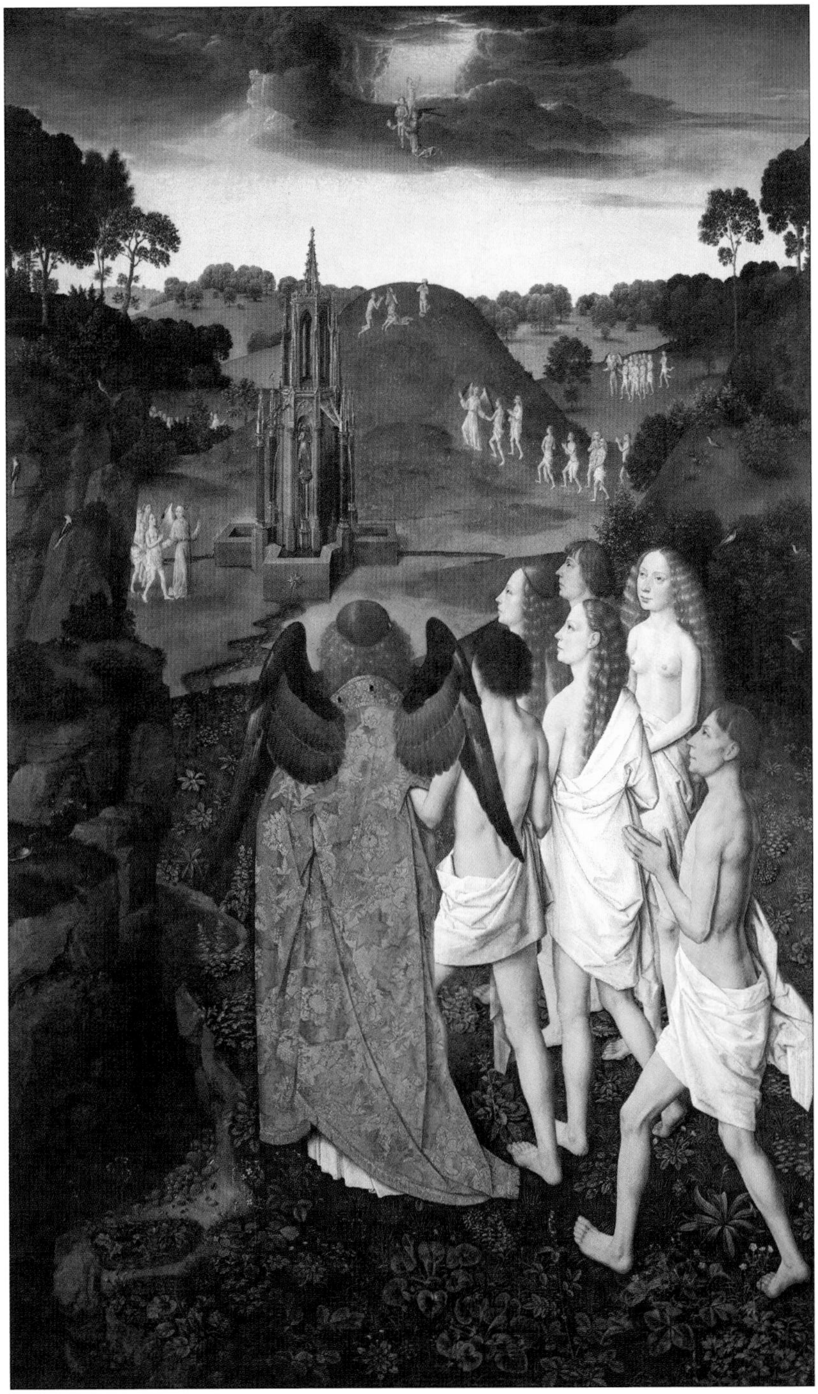

Bouts often gave his religious works beautiful landscape backgrounds, as in this side wing of the triptych* The Last Judgment *(c.1468).

Memlinc, who had been born near Frankfurt in central Germany but who became a citizen of Bruges in 1465. To judge from the city's tax records, he ended his life as one of its wealthiest residents. Commissions flowed in not just from the Netherlands but also from France, England, and Italy.

Schools and Movements

The Bruges School

Like their counterparts in Italy, Flemish painters tended to gather in specific cities where distinctive traditions of painterly skills passed down from generation to generation. Although it now lies inland, Bruges (in modern-day western Belgium) was an important river port in the 15th century, serving as the capital of the ruling dukes of Burgundy.

The wealth that came from the wool trade supported a school of painters that traced its origins to Jan van Eyck (c.1390–1441), who spent the last decade of his life in the city. After van Eyck's death in 1441, Petrus Christus (c.1410–75/6), Hans Memlinc (c.1430/40–94)—who moved to Bruges from Germany—and Gerard David (c.1460–1523) all continued to work in the manner he had established. The paintings these masters produced were mostly calm devotional works marked by tenderness and gentle piety, notable for their rich color and delicate handling of light.

The school came to an end, along with Bruges's prosperity, at the end of the 15th century, when the river connecting the city to the North Sea silted up. Antwerp later took its place as an artistic and commercial center.

Memlinc and van der Goes

Memlinc owed his success to the widespread appeal of his paintings, which treated familiar, mostly religious themes in an uncontroversial way designed to appeal to wealthy townsfolk. What distinguishes works such as *Allegory of Chastity* (1475), in which two heraldic lions guard a virgin from unwanted suitors, is a delicacy of tone and a limpid portrayal of light, shown casting its glow over a meticulously rendered vista of a distant city and hills. Like most of the great Flemish artists, he was also a first-rate portraitist with a gift for capturing the personality of his sitters.

Memlinc's art is occasionally (perhaps unfairly) accused of being insipid, a charge that could hardly be made against his contemporary Hugo van der Goes. He spent his life in Ghent, where his career was as tragic as Memlinc's was successful.

A painter of huge talent, van der Goes specialized in big works featuring life-size figures—his best-known work, the Portinari Altarpiece (c.1475–76), stands 9 feet (2.75 m) high and measures 18 feet (5.5m) across its three panels. Yet he also painted some of the loveliest of all Flemish landscape backgrounds, employing precise brushstrokes that seem to enumerate every branch of every tree. Despite his artistic success—he was elected dean of the guild of painters in

Ghent in 1474—he started drinking heavily and fell into a clinical depression, characterized by fears of not being able to complete his works. He was eventually hospitalized in a monastery near Brussels, where he died insane in 1482.

Van der Goes rivaled van der Weyden in his ability to create large-scale works with a strong emotional punch. Paintings such as *The Adoration of the Shepherds* (the central panel of the Portinari Altarpiece) not only convey the awful solemnity of the scene but, in the figures of the praying shepherds, also reveal a gift for characterization that few other masters of the time could rival.

THE ANTWERP SCHOOL

By the end of the 15th century the river port of Bruges was silting up and trade, patronage, and art all moved farther

The center panel of Van der Goes's Portinari Altarpiece represents the Virgin kneeling in adoration before the newborn Christ, attended by shepherds and angels.

Massys's fondness for everyday detail can be seen in such paintings as **The Moneychanger and His Wife** *(c.1514).*

inland to Antwerp on the Scheldt River. One of the founders of the Antwerp School was Quentin Massys (c.1466–1530), who had learned his art in his home town of Leuven, where he studied the work of Dierec Bouts. Legend has it that he gave up a career as a metalsmith to become an artist through love of a painter's daughter, hoping to impress her father with his skill.

It proved a good career move, for he became a popular and prolific artist, excelling at both portraits and religious subjects. His paintings introduced a new element of sophistication to the Flemish tradition, partly imported from Italian art. One marked trait in his work was an eye for everyday detail that prepared the way for the later Dutch fashion for genre painting (canvases showing ordinary people in workaday settings). Massys also had a taste for the grotesque, seen in such works as *The Ugly Duchess* (1525–30).

Several of Massys's paintings feature background scenes of fantastic wooded mountains—a speciality of the painter Joachim Patinir (c.1480–1524), who is known to have collaborated with Massys. Patinir was possibly the first painter to specialize in landscapes; when human figures appear in his works, they are almost completely subordinate to the natural world, which often has a fantastic quality, with jagged rocks, picturesque ruins, and cool blue distances. Patinir's skills were admired by Albrecht Dürer, who attended his wedding and drew his portrait.

BOSCH

Most of the Netherlands masters worked in the southern provinces that would become Belgium, but one of the greatest came from the Dutch lands to the north. This was Hieronymus Bosch (c.1450–1516), who took his name from his home town 's-Hertogenbosch. The town was devastated by a terrible fire in 1463 when the painter was about 13 years old, and it is possible that the taste for flames and infernos that appears in his later work was influenced by childhood memories of this catastrophe.

Bosch's **Garden of Earthly Delights** *is thought to have been commissioned by Count Hendrik III of Nassau for his castle in Brussels.*

Masterpiece

Heaven and Hell

The Dutch artist Hieronymus Bosch (c.1450–1516) is famous now for his surrealistic canvases that reveal a riotous visual imagination, but in earlier times he had a reputation as a deeply religious artist. Several of his works take the form of triptychs, including *The Garden of Earthly Delights* (c.1510), which exemplifies the startling imagery and curious symbolism for which Bosch is known.

The painting depicts four views of the world. When the side panels are closed over the central image, the outer panels are revealed. They show a representation of the newly created world (a flat Earth within a celestial sphere). When the side panels are opened out (as here), the Garden of Eden is seen on the left; God unites Adam and Eve to live in harmony with nature. On the right is a powerful depiction of the torments of Hell. The central panel shows a more fantastical place than Earth and contains elements of Paradise and Hell.

Human folly was a favorite theme for Bosch. Here he seems to be warning against the pleasures of the flesh. Demons have encroached upon the central panel, either to encourage the humans into sexual acts or to torment them because of their unrestrained behavior. The right-hand panel is a reminder of where it will all end—Bosch seems to be issuing a warning to the wicked (who seem here to include humanity in general).

The imposing effect of the subject of Fouquet's **Portrait of Guillaume Juvenal des Ursins** *is enhanced by the framing of the subject's head in the sumptuous red and gold background.*

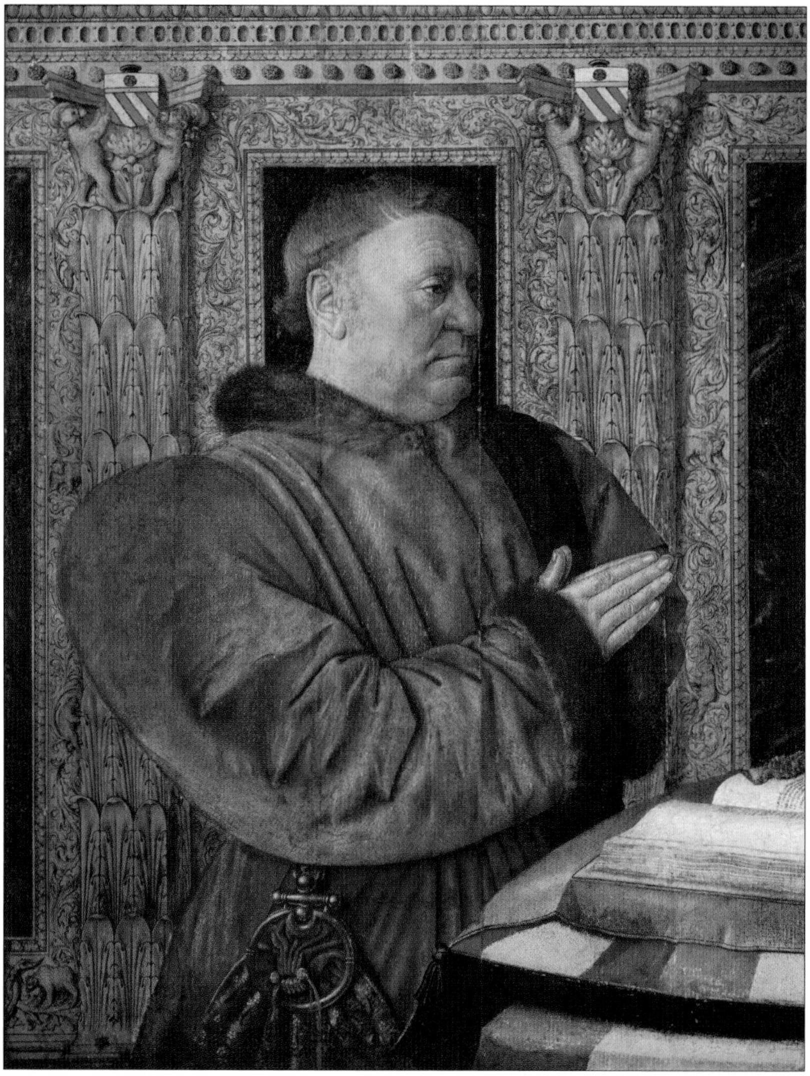

What is certain is that Bosch brought an extraordinary visual imagination to illustrating the fears and horrors that haunted late medieval minds. Many artists, particularly in the northern lands, portrayed the demons and fiends with which hellfire preachers threatened sinners in sermons at the time, but none visualized them with anything like the energy and precision that Bosch brought to the task.

As a skilled artisan Bosch mastered the Renaissance techniques of perspective and composition, but he appears to have had no sympathy for the humanist message of human potential. Rather, the individuals in his paintings are fools trapped within their vices. They have little to hope for but the punishment of the damned. In imagining their fate, he showed a surrealistic vision that today could have brought him a career as a computer-game designer.

FLEMISH INFLUENCE IN FRANCE AND SPAIN

The array of talent on display in the Flemish cities inevitably had a knock-on effect on the art of the surrounding lands. French painters of the time were torn between the Flemish influence and that of the Italian artists to the south.

Jean Fouquet, the greatest French artist of the day, worked in the northern city of Tours (where he ended up as court painter) but traveled to Italy as a young man. There he learned to graft Italian techniques onto a style honed by working as a miniaturist. Among other talents, Fouquet excelled at realistic portraiture, as shown by his *Portrait of Guillaume Juvenal des Ursins* (c.1455), a powerful bishop who served as chancellor to two French kings.

Other French artists of the time were less directly exposed to the Italian

The Villeneuve-lès-Avignon Pietà *is dominated by the suffering of the central figure of the Virgin. The painting has profound emotional and dramatic force, and is one of the finest representations in existence of the death of Christ.*

spirit. The artist long known as the Master of Moulins, because his chief surviving work is a triptych in Moulins Cathedral in central France, is a case in point. Now often identified with a painter named Jean Hey (known to have been active in the last two decades of the 15th century), he painted stately religious works in a style that owed much to Hugo van der Goes.

The anonymous *Pietà* (c.1455), which some call the greatest French painting of the 15th century, was even less Italian in its inspiration, even though it was commissioned for the church of Villeneuve-lès-Avignon, not far from the Italian border. Its tortured vision of the dead Christ seems rather to herald the German master Matthias Grünewald, whose masterworks it predated by some 50 years.

Links between Flanders and the Spanish court ensured that Flemish painting was also influential in Spain. Jan van Eyck himself visited Spain and Portugal in the 1420s on business for the duke of Burgundy. His work had a profound effect on artists such as Bartolomé Bermejo (c.1440–c.98), who brought a portentous and very Spanish

TOOLS AND TECHNIQUES

Woodcuts and Engravings

About 50 years before Johannes Gutenberg (c.1398–c.1468) pioneered movable-type printing, artists were producing woodcuts—the first appeared in about the year 1400. The process involved putting printer's ink on a block of wood and pressing it onto paper. A flat surface would have produced a plain black rectangle, but lines cut in the wood appeared white, enabling artists who were also skilled woodworkers to produce black-and-white images. These could be reproduced many times simply by reapplying the ink to the block and pressing it on fresh sheets of paper.

Just as woodblocks developed out of the art of woodworking, metal engraving was an extension of the skills of gold- and silversmiths. The craftsmen cut designs into sheets of metal, most often copper (used for so-called copperplate engraving). In the opposite way to woodcuts, untouched surfaces of the metal printed white, while the ink in the incised lines came out black. The first metal engravings appeared about 30 years after woodcuts.

Both techniques became hugely popular with artists across much of Europe. One reason was the close link between metal- and woodworking and the fine arts; many painters in Renaissance times also doubled as wood carvers and metalsmiths. Yet the techniques proved particularly significant in Germany, where there were comparatively few patrons willing to spend lavishly on commissions. As a result, generations of artists found it easier and more profitable to sell limited editions of prints to several buyers rather than devote months of effort to creating a single, unique painting.

grandeur to works such as the *Piedad Desplà* (1490) now in Barcelona Cathedral.

Pedro Berruguete (c.1450–c.1504), Bermejo's contemporary, began his career very much under Flemish influence but later traveled to Italy, where he worked for a time in the ducal palace at Urbino. He subsequently returned to Spain and became court painter to Ferdinand I (1442–1516) and Isabella (1451–1504).

Dürer's dramatic woodcut* The Four Horsemen of the Apocalypse *(1498) radiates with intense, Gothic fantasy.

 See also: The High Renaissance in Italy **28–49**

A GOLDEN AGE IN GERMANY

Of all the European nations Germany was unique in using the Flemish influence as a springboard to create its own distinctive national style. So successful were its artists that they spawned a golden age of German painting in the years 1500 to 1525, when the High Renaissance in Italy was also reaching its peak.

One reason why German artists went their own way was technological. It was in Germany that Johannes Gutenberg (c.1398–c.1468) introduced movable-type printing, previously known only in China. Even before Gutenberg applied his ingenuity to the production of books, artists had been using the woodblock technique to produce prints (see box opposite). From about 1440 metalsmiths used their talents to produce copperplate engravings, which in the hands of great artists produced even finer results.

The new techniques were taken up enthusiastically by artists, partly because they enabled them to reach a wide audience—prints, unlike paintings, could be mechanically reproduced—but also for want of other outlets. Although Germany had cities and a growing mercantile economy of its own, it lacked the tight urban network found in Flanders or northern Italy. In 15th–century Germany patrons, whether in the form of individual nobles or municipalities, were relatively hard to find.

The **Death of the Virgin** *is tenderly depicted by Stoss in this detail from the central panel of the high altar of the Church of St. Mary in Cracow.*

GERMAN SCULPTURE AND ENGRAVING

As a result, the German tradition in art was partly nurtured outside the field of painting. Sculpture continued to be important, producing a tortured genius of its own in the shape of Veit Stoss (c.1450–1533). Stoss did some of his finest work in the Polish city of Cracow, but he

Grünewald painted numerous versions of the Crucifixion. In the Isenheim Altarpiece (above), he created a vision of the scene that was unique in his time by focusing on the human suffering of Christ rather than the glory of His divine sacrifice.

returned to his home town of Nuremberg in 1496. Robbed of his savings, he attempted to regain them by forging a document, for which he was convicted and branded on both cheeks in 1503. He later received a pardon from the emperor, but nonetheless spent his last years as an embittered man. Something of his inner torment comes over in his dramatic figures swathed in contorted drapery.

Otherwise, the German style was largely incubated in the work of engravers, from Master E. S. (a 15th-century engraver known only by the monogram on several of his prints) through the multitalented Martin Schongauer (c.1440–91). Few of Schongauer's paintings survive, but at least 115 engravings are known to be by his hand. Schongauer's importance in the development of engraving lay in bringing a painter's eye to an art that had previously been dominated by craftsmen. His prints have a grace and subtlety that matches and even exceeds that of the best masters' drawings of his day.

It was only fitting that the greatest German Renaissance artist, Albrecht Dürer, should have traveled as a young man in 1492 to Schongauer's home town of Colmar in Alsace to pay him homage. He arrived too late: Schongauer was already dead. Even so, Dürer learned from Schongauer's example, doing much of his own finest work in the form of woodcuts and engravings.

Schools and Movements

The Danube School

A group of German and Austrian artists at work around the year 1500 made landscape a central feature of their work. They took their inspiration from the beauty of the lands around the Danube River. The groundwork for the movement was prepared by artists from the Tyrol region of Austria, notably Michael Pacher (c.1435–98) and Rueland Frueauf the Elder (c.1440/45–1507), but it reached maturity in the paintings of Albrecht Altdorfer (c.1480–1538), Wolf Huber (c.1480/90–1553), and Lucas Cranach (1472–1553). What was new in their work was not just the fresh prominence given to landscape but also the way in which it was made to reflect the emotions of the human figures in a way that prefigured 19th-century Romanticism.

Grünewald and Cranach

Dürer's international vision contrasted sharply with the specifically German expressionism (the expression of human emotions in painting) of his greatest contemporary, known to art history as Matthias Grünewald. It seems likely, however, that this was not his real name; he signed his painting M. G. N., and a painter named Mathis Gothardt Nithardt is known to have been active in his home region at the time. Whatever his true identity, the master left very few works. Those that survived take the form of altarpieces painted for provincial churches, suggesting that he lived the life of a traditional journeyman painter in the medieval manner.

What was new in Grünewald's paintings, however, was a passionate intensity allied to a technique honed on all the skills of the Renaissance masters. No other painter has ever captured the horror of Christ's crucifixion as he did in his apocalyptic Isenheim Altarpiece (c.1515) for the hospital chapel of a monastery in Alsace. Yet his image of the Resurrection in the same work shows that he had equal visionary power in depicting the positive side of the Passion.

Grunewald's career as a solitary genius could hardly have been more different from that of the third of the masters who came to artistic maturity at the turn of the 16th century. Lucas Cranach (1472–1553) was a career artist, immensely popular in his day, who

Cranach's* Rest On the Flight into Egypt *(1504) shows the Holy Family against a German pine-forest landscape.

flourished under the patronage of the elector of Saxony. From brilliant beginnings painting sparklingly fresh landscapes in the style of the Danube School (see box on page 65), he in time turned into a court painter, always charming but no longer innovative or challenging. In his later works it is hard to distinguish his own hand from that of the many apprentices who populated his studio. Yet his vast range was unmatched, stretching from portraits through some of the earliest northern nudes to humorous grotesques including a lost canvas of hares capturing and roasting huntsmen.

Holbein

Hans Holbein (c.1497–1543) belonged to the generation after Cranach, Grünewald, and Dürer, and his work showed even greater visual sophistication. Few individuals in art history have matched him for sheer technical virtuosity. Brought up in Augsburg, he went abroad to build his career, first in Switzerland and then as court painter to Henry VIII (1491–1547) of England.

There he developed a unique portrait style that involved making detailed, full-size sketches in pencil, ink, and colored chalk and then transferring the image to canvas via a form of carbon paper. His *Portrait of George Gisze* (1532), a German merchant in London, shows his extraordinary skill at rendering textures and perspective effects as well as his intense gift of characterization.

Holbein died of plague in England in 1543, and with him the great age of German painting came to an end. The profound social and religious rift known as the Reformation was at least partly responsible for its demise. The cause of the reformers (who were protesting against abuses within the Catholic Church) was supported by most artists at the time, including Dürer, Cranach, Grünewald, and Holbein.

Over time, though, the disruption caused as Germany split between Catholic and Protestant states proved unfavorable for art. As early as 1524 discontented farm laborers rose against their masters in the Peasants' War, cloaking deep-seated economic grievances in the guise of religious protest. For the next 125 years Germany was split by political and religious divisions, culminating in the 17th century in the horrors of the Thirty Years' War.

Meanwhile artists, however sympathetic to the reformers' cause, lost commissions as extreme Protestants turned against display and show, preferring unadorned chapels and meeting places to churches rich with paintings and painted sculptures. Germany continued to produce talented artists, but in the fractured society of the later 16th and 17th centuries they found it hard to prosper.

Holbein's* Portrait of George Gisze. *During his long visit to England, beginning in 1532, Holbein painted a series of portraits of German merchants working in London's commercial community—probably for their families back in Germany.

INSIDE THE ARTIST

Albrecht Dürer

Of all the German artists of his day, Albrecht Dürer (1471–1528) was the true Renaissance man. He had a wide-ranging intellectual curiosity that led him in later life to write theoretical treatises on pictorial composition and on mathematics.

As a young man he was apprenticed to a painter and book illustrator, and gained experience in painting and woodcuts. His talent quickly flourished, and at the age of 19 he produced a remarkable painting of his father, *Albrecht Dürer the Elder* (1490). He traveled to Italy twice and established cordial relations with his fellow masters there—he and Raphael (1483–1520) even exchanged drawings. In Antwerp, which he visited in later life, he was greeted as a master and honored with a civic banquet.

Artistically, his tastes were wide, extending to the first Aztec artefacts to reach Europe after the Spanish conquest of Mexico in 1521, of which he wrote: "I have seen nothing that has so rejoiced my heart as these things, for I saw in them strange and exquisitely worked objects, and marveled at the subtle genius of men in distant lands."

Dürer painted relatively few canvases, but they include a sequence of three self-portraits completed when he was in his 20s. The unflinching work shown opposite—the third and final self-portrait—was made in 1500, when he was 28 years old. In it he chose to show himself face-on, gazing directly into the eyes of the viewer. The long hair and the raised hand recall images of Jesus Christ.

Dürer was living at the time in his home town of Nuremberg, having returned from a trip to Italy four years earlier. During his travels he had stayed in Venice, where he studied the work of Andrea Mantegna (c.1431–1506) and met Giovanni Bellini (1430–1516). The Italian experience had profoundly affected him, not least by encouraging him to take a more theoretical approach to his art. His interest in mathematical proportion is revealed in the careful planning of this portrait, in which the length of the head exactly matches the distance from the beard to the pointing finger.

Such calculations were in vogue at a time when in Italy Fra Luca di Pacioli was preparing his work on the Golden Section (see box on page 35) and Leonardo da Vinci was producing his famous studies of the proportions of the human body.

Yet this self-portrait also suggests Dürer's religious convictions. The resemblance to Christ may have had particular significance for a work that was painted on the eve of the year 1500, the dawn of a new century, when many people expected Jesus' second coming. The Latin tag on the right of the painting translates as, "I, Albrecht Dürer of Noricum [the Roman name for southern Germany], portrayed myself thus with my own colors at the age of 28."

Dürer was one of his own favorite subjects. His earliest self-portrait was a drawing made at the age of 13.* Self-Portrait at 28 *(1500), shown here, was his last-known painted self-portrait.

 See also: The High Renaissance in Italy **28–49**

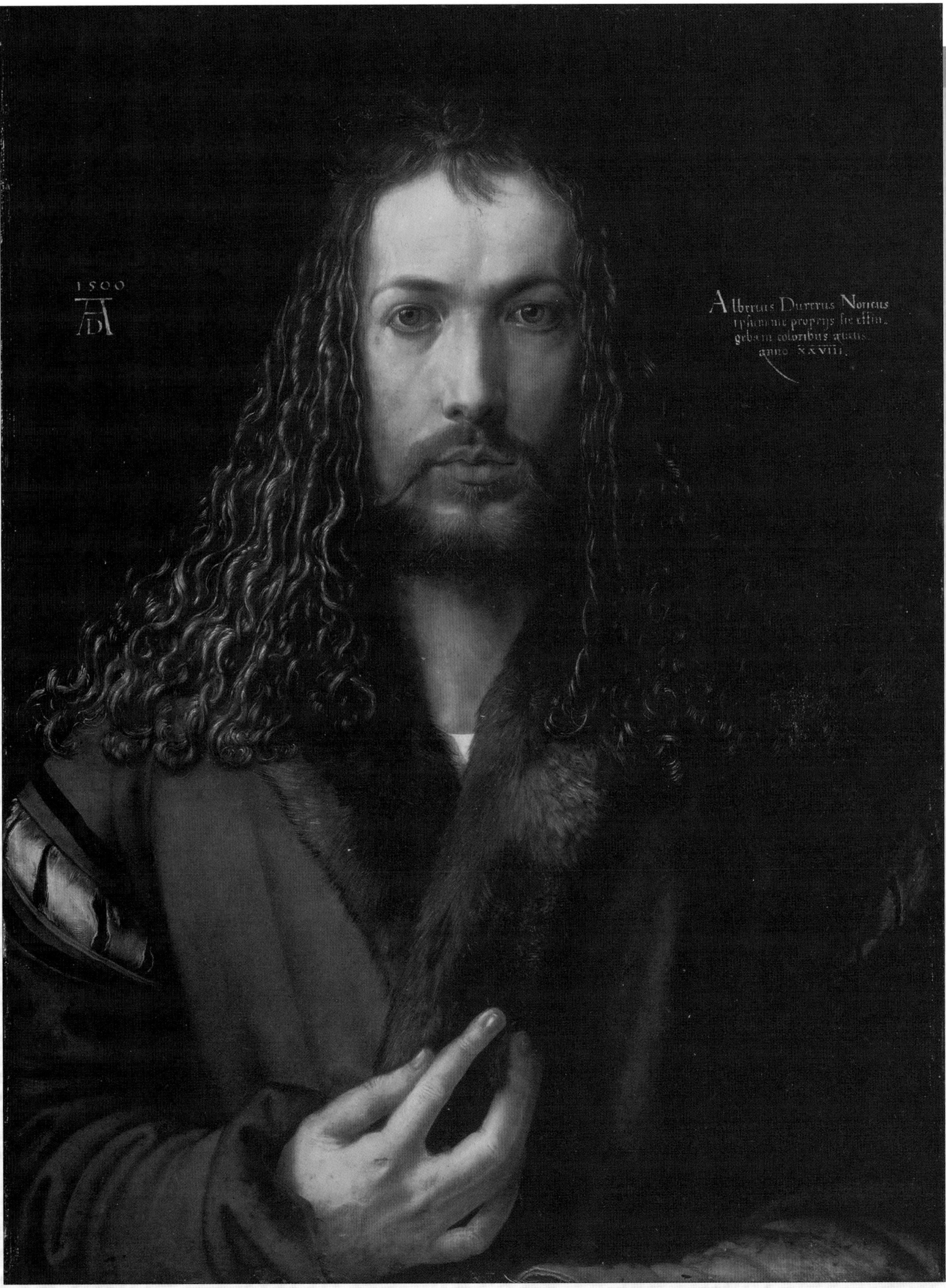
1500
Albertus Durerus Noricus
ipsum me propriis sic effin-
gebam coloribus aetatis
anno XXVIII.

1525–1575

The Late Renaissance and Mannerism

Three decades of warfare in northern Italy culminated with the Sack of Rome in 1527, marking the end of the High Renaissance years. The decades after 1527 were very different from what had gone before and seemed an age away from the optimistic time of the late 15th century. As artists began to drift away from Rome, the cultural atmosphere that had nurtured the talents of Raphael and Leonardo was dispersed. A new style of painting known as Mannerism gradually appeared; characterized by distortion and exaggeration yet brimming with energy, it would last until the advent of Baroque art.

In May 1527, German troops of the Holy Roman Emperor Charles V (1500–58) seized the city of Rome and subjected it to more than a month of destruction and pillage. The last Florentine republic collapsed in 1530, when the Medici dukes established despotic rule. Five years later Milan fell to the Spanish branch of the Hapsburg Dynasty, which already ruled southern Italy. Only the Papal States and Venice maintained real independence. Over thirty years of warfare in northern Italy had disrupted trade and spread devastation on a wide scale.

By the mid-16th century Italy's economy was also in decline. The downturn was caused in part by inflation sweeping across Europe as a result of an influx of silver from New World mines following the discovery of the Americas. In addition, new sea passages around Africa to India and East Asia bypassed the Mediterranean, meaning less trade for Italian ports.

REFORMATION AND COUNTER-REFORMATION

Another crucial factor disrupting the Renaissance world was the spread of religious discord. The Reformation—started in Germany when the priest Martin Luther (1483–1546) posted his 95 Theses on the door of Wittenberg Church in 1517—split the Christian world between Catholic and Protestant factions. One

 See also: The High Renaissance in Italy **28–49**

immediate result was a reduction in church funds for the arts. One of Luther's main complaints against the Papacy concerned the sale of "indulgences" (promising pardon for sins in return for cash payments). The indulgences had been sold to finance the rebuilding of St. Peter's Basilica in Rome, a project headed at the time by the painter Raphael (1483–1520).

The Catholic reform movement, known as the Counter-Reformation, effectively cleaned up such abuses. But it also ushered in a new age of enforced orthodoxy, which ran counter to the spirit of free intellectual enquiry the Renaissance had encouraged. By the later 16th century the individual no longer seemed the supreme master of his or her own fate.

THE ARTISTIC CHALLENGE

Even at the time, the High Renaissance years from 1500 to 1525 were seen as the pinnacle of artistic achievement. The theoretical problems of perspective and space composition that had bedeviled painters in the 15th century had been resolved. The Renaissance masters—Leonardo da Vinci (1452–1519), Raphael, Michelangelo (1475–1564), and Titian (c.1485–1576)—had produced works of unsurpassed harmony and balance.

The problem for the rising generation of artists was what to do next? There was little to be gained by simply imitating their elders—they would probably only produce inferior versions of work that had already been done better. Like creative people in every age, they wanted to go beyond the masters who had taught them.

Artists responded in varying ways. One who felt the rising tide of Catholic fervor was Fra Bartolommeo (1472–1517), inspired by the brief dictatorship of the religious and political reformer Girolamo Savonarola (1452–98) in Florence in the

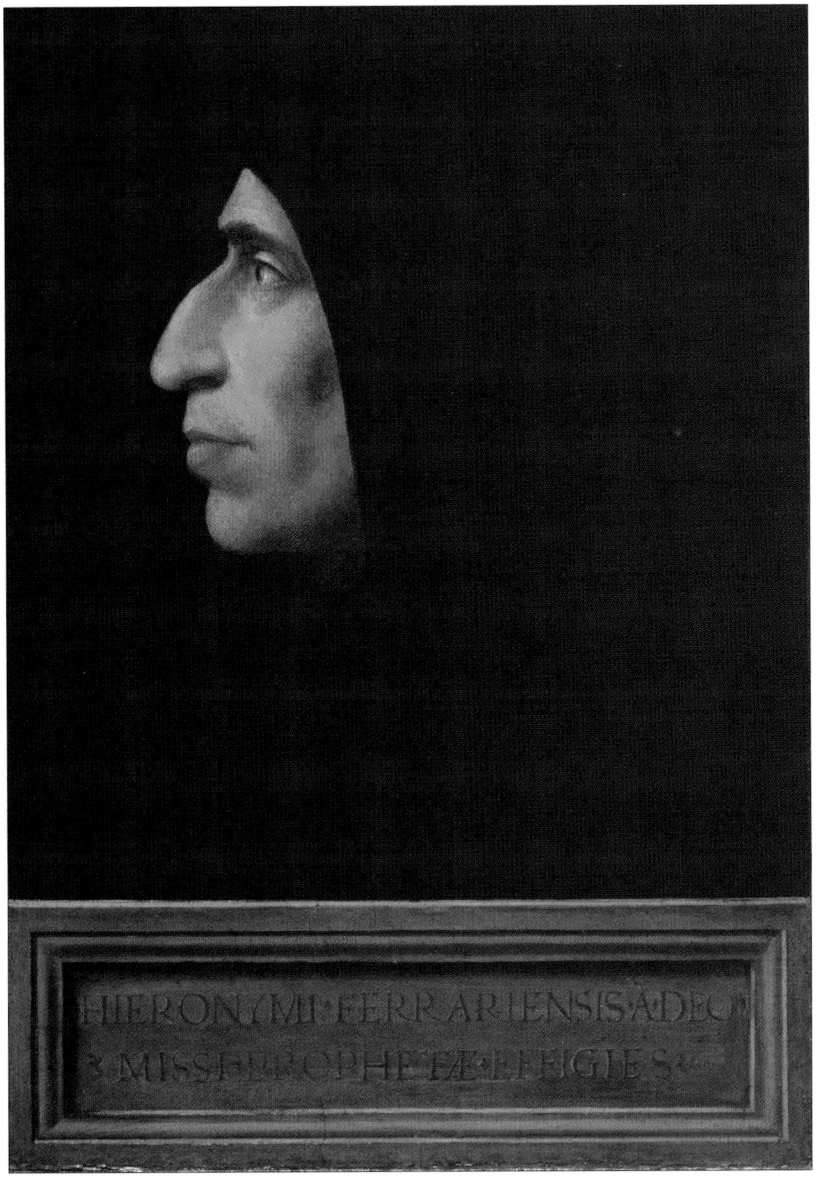

Portrait of Girolamo Savonarola ***by Fra Bartolommeo (c.1498). Savonarola's denunciations of the worldliness and corruption of art greatly influenced the artist, who took up holy orders and even gave up painting for a while.***

1490s. Bartolommeo was in the Convent of San Marco in 1498 when it was stormed and Savonarola was dragged off to be imprisoned and later burned at the stake. Bartolommeo became a monk ("Fra" means "Brother") and ended up as head of the monastery workshop. He developed a new style of pious art, introducing figures with rapt expressions, dramatic gestures, and swirling clouds of angels—all traits developed in the Late Renaissance period that subsequently fed into the Baroque style of the 17th century.

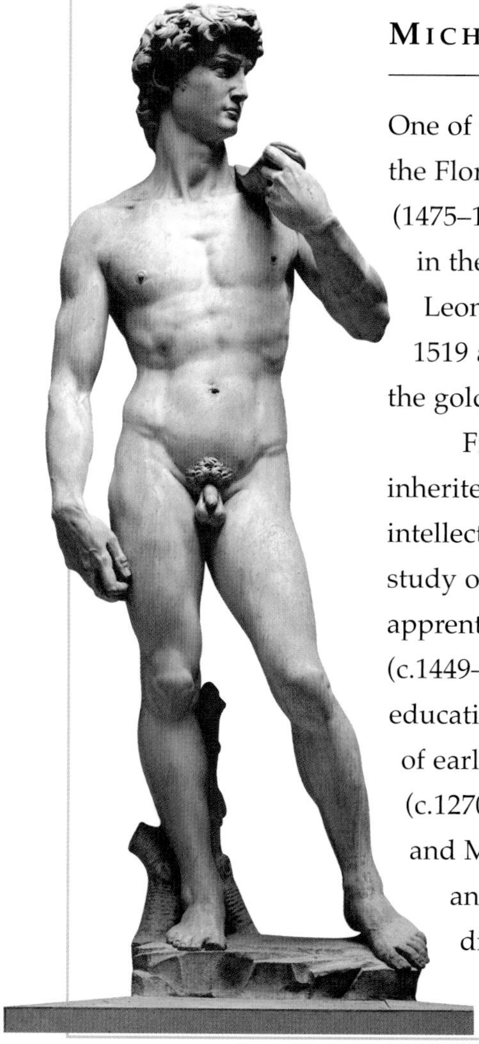

Michelangelo's* David *shows the young David about to fight the giant Goliath. His face, with its furrowed brow and tense expression, adds a dramatic psychological dimension rarely seen before in sculpture.

MICHELANGELO

One of the great geniuses of world art, the Florentine Michelangelo Buonarroti (1475–1564) came to artistic maturity in the High Renaissance. But unlike Leonardo and Raphael, who died in 1519 and 1520 respectively, he outlived the golden age and was 89 when he died.

From his early years Michelangelo inherited the Florentine tradition of an intellectual art based primarily on the study of the human form. He was apprenticed to Domenico Ghirlandaio (c.1449–94), but most of his artistic education came from his own studies of earlier masters such as Giotto (c.1270–1337), Donatello (c.1386–1466), and Masaccio (1401–28/29) and from anatomical research gained by dissecting corpses as well as drawing nudes.

Michelangelo first came to prominence as a sculptor. His *Pietà* (1498–99) of Mary with the body of the dead Christ, created for the Vatican, and his *David* (1501–04), commissioned by the Wool Guild in Florence, were completed by the time he was 30 and were both recognized as masterpieces, a reputation they have kept to this day.

 See also: The Pre- and Early Renaissance 8–27

THE SISTINE CHAPEL CEILING

Michelangelo's enduring fame as a painter sprang from one of the most daunting commissions an artist could receive. Pope Julius II (1443–1513) wanted a painter to decorate the ceiling of the Sistine Chapel in the Vatican. The walls of the chapel were already covered with works by leading artists of the previous century, including Botticelli (c.1445–1510) and Ghirlandaio.

Michelangelo labored on the project for four years, standing on scaffolding and constantly peering upward as he painted; he only saw the overall effect of his work on breaks or at the end of each day. The effort gave

Michelangelo made about 300 drawings for the Sistine Chapel ceiling. They were enlarged and transferred to the ceiling, and he then began the arduous task of painting.

him back pain for the rest of his life, but the result was a triumph. The completed work included more than 300 individual figures and some iconic scenes—in particular, the image of God stretching out his hand to give Adam life is world-famous.

Completed in 1512 when Michelangelo was 37, the Sistine Chapel ceiling confirmed his position as the supreme artist of his age. From that time on people took to calling him *Il Divino* ("the divine one"), and critics spoke of the *terribilità* ("terrible awe") his work inspired.

For all the adulation he received, the second half of Michelangelo's life was not a happy time. He was well aware that he had lived on beyond the golden age, and as he grew older his mood darkened, as evidenced by the controversy over his painting of *The Last Judgment* (1536–41) (see pages 88 to 89).

Even in his final years, however, Michelangelo notched up many outstanding achievements, particularly in architecture: For example, he designed the dome of St. Peter's Basilica, one of the best-known landmarks of the Christian world. His sculptural style also continued to evolve. In his final work, the Rondanini *Pietà* (c.1552–64), he turned his back on the colossal torsos he had favored since his *David* 50 years before, choosing instead a deliberately rough and unfinished manner in which to express Mary's grief.

MANNERISM

If even the supremely gifted Michelangelo sometimes slipped into excess in his later years, his followers proved still more eager to go to extremes. The result was Mannerism, a style of art that strayed beyond the balancing point of harmony into discord and exaggeration. At its worst Mannerist art degenerated into self-parody, but at its best it produced works of great virtuosity and nervous energy.

TOOLS AND TECHNIQUES

Sotto in Sù

Meaning literally "from below upward" in Italian, *sotto in sù* is a technique that employs extreme perspective effects to show figures on a ceiling or a dome so that viewers feel the images are floating above them. The device was first used by Andrea Mantegna (c.1431–1506) in Mantua in the 1470s as an extension of his experiments with foreshortening. Correggio (c.1490–1534) employed it to dramatic effect 50 years later in the dome of Parma Cathedral, attracting criticism from some individuals at the time—one church canon spoke dismissively of "a hash of frogs' legs" dangling over the congregation. By the 17th century, people had got used to the effect, and it became a standard part of the Baroque repertory.

Romano's **Fall of the Giants** *depicts the mythical battle between the Greek gods and the giants. The image shows Zeus, thunderbolt in hand, descending from his throne to confront the rebellious giants.*

Of all the classical masters, Raphael was the most noted for his calm perfection, but it was his most gifted pupil, Giulio Romano (?1499–1546), who subsequently pushed the limits the furthest. Romano, who had completed some of Raphael's unfinished works after the master's death in 1520, was commissioned in the 1530s to decorate the Palazzo del Tè for the Gonzaga dukes of Mantua. There he sought to outdo Michelangelo in portraying contorted muscular figures in dynamic action, covering an entire room of the palace with a spectacular vision of the *Fall of the Giants*. His goal was to overwhelm the viewer with the force of his vision.

Another artist who sought to impress by muscle power was Rosso Fiorentino (1494–1540). Rosso left his native Florence for Rome in the 1520s. During the sack of the city in 1527, he was captured by German soldiers who stripped him of his clothes. After this alarming experience he traveled around Italy until 1530, when he went to France at the invitation of Francis I (1494–1547). There he became the first leader of the School of Fontainebleau (see box below).

Rosso's works express a sense of tense emotion as much by the fractured nature of their surfaces, which seems almost to prefigure Cubism, as through their powerful male figures. He was a devotee of *contrapposto*—an Italian word used to describe figures in which the torso and lower body are shown twisting in opposite directions. The sense of unease that his works convey found expression in elaborate symbolism and allegory as well as in the contorted postures of his subjects.

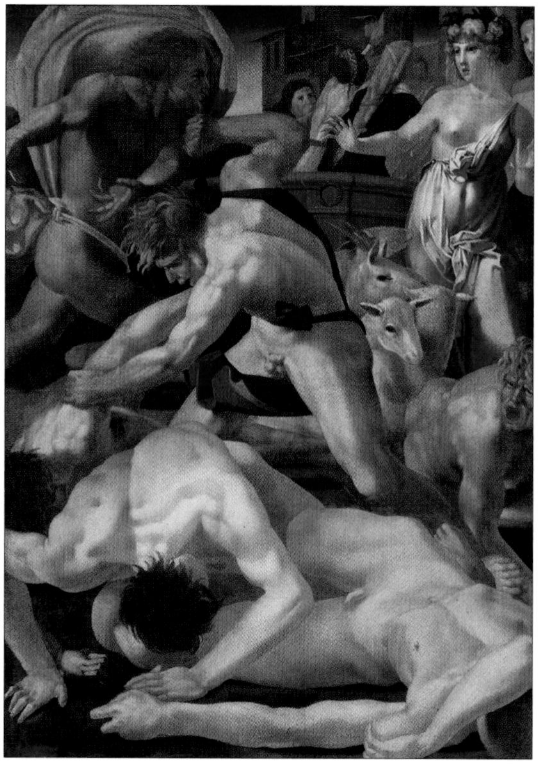

***The nude figures that dominate Rosso's* Moses Defending the Daughters of Jethro *(1523–24) reflect the artist's enthusiasm for* contrapposto.**

SCHOOLS AND MOVEMENTS

The School of Fontainebleau

The School of Fontainebleau was an oddity in art history, since, although it was based in France, its foremost artists were Italian. The school had its origins in the French king's desire to make his court a "second Rome." A model Renaissance ruler, Francis I (1494–1547) was a lavish patron of the arts. Needing painters and sculptors to decorate his palaces—particularly the château of Fontainebleau 35 miles (55 km) south of Paris—he looked to Italy to supply them. From 1530 on, he spent large sums of money enticing leading Mannerists such as Rosso Fiorentino (1494–1540) and Primaticcio (c.1504–70) to work in France. The sculptor and goldsmith Benvenuto Cellini (1500–71) arrived in 1537, and Niccoló dell' Abbate (c.1510–71) came in 1552.

The style that the Italians perfected in France was elegant and refined, devoted above all to the idealization of the female form. Its most direct influence on French art was in the field of sculpture, in which the Frenchmen Jean Goujon (c.1510–?68) and Germaine Pilon (c.1525–90) developed a graceful and sensuous approach that mirrored the decorative manner pioneered at court.

PONTORMO AND BRONZINO

In his early years, Rosso had studied under Andrea del Sarto (1486–1530) in Florence. One of his fellow pupils was

MASTERPIECE

Madonna with the Long Neck

Born Girolamo Francesco Mazzola, Parmigianino (1503–40) owed his nickname to his hometown of Parma. Captured in the Sack of Rome in 1527, he returned to Parma after his release. There he grew increasingly eccentric. According to the biographer Giorgio Vasari (1511–74), he became obsessed by alchemy—the pseudoscience of trying to change base metals into gold—and "changed from the gentle and fastidious man he had been into an almost wild figure with a beard and long, straggling locks."

In his short life he painted some of the most refined of all Mannerist works. *Madonna with the Long Neck* (c.1535) is one of the best examples. Its unbalanced composition, with a crowd of figures on one side and an enigmatic single column on the other, is typical of the movement. So is the contrast in size between the large figure of the Madonna and the tiny John the Baptist seen in the right-hand corner.

The long neck and small head of the main figure, and the huge size of the infant Jesus are also typical of the games the Mannerists liked to play with scale. Yet the combined effect is one of grace and elegance. The painting's oddities fall away before its warmth and sophisticated beauty.

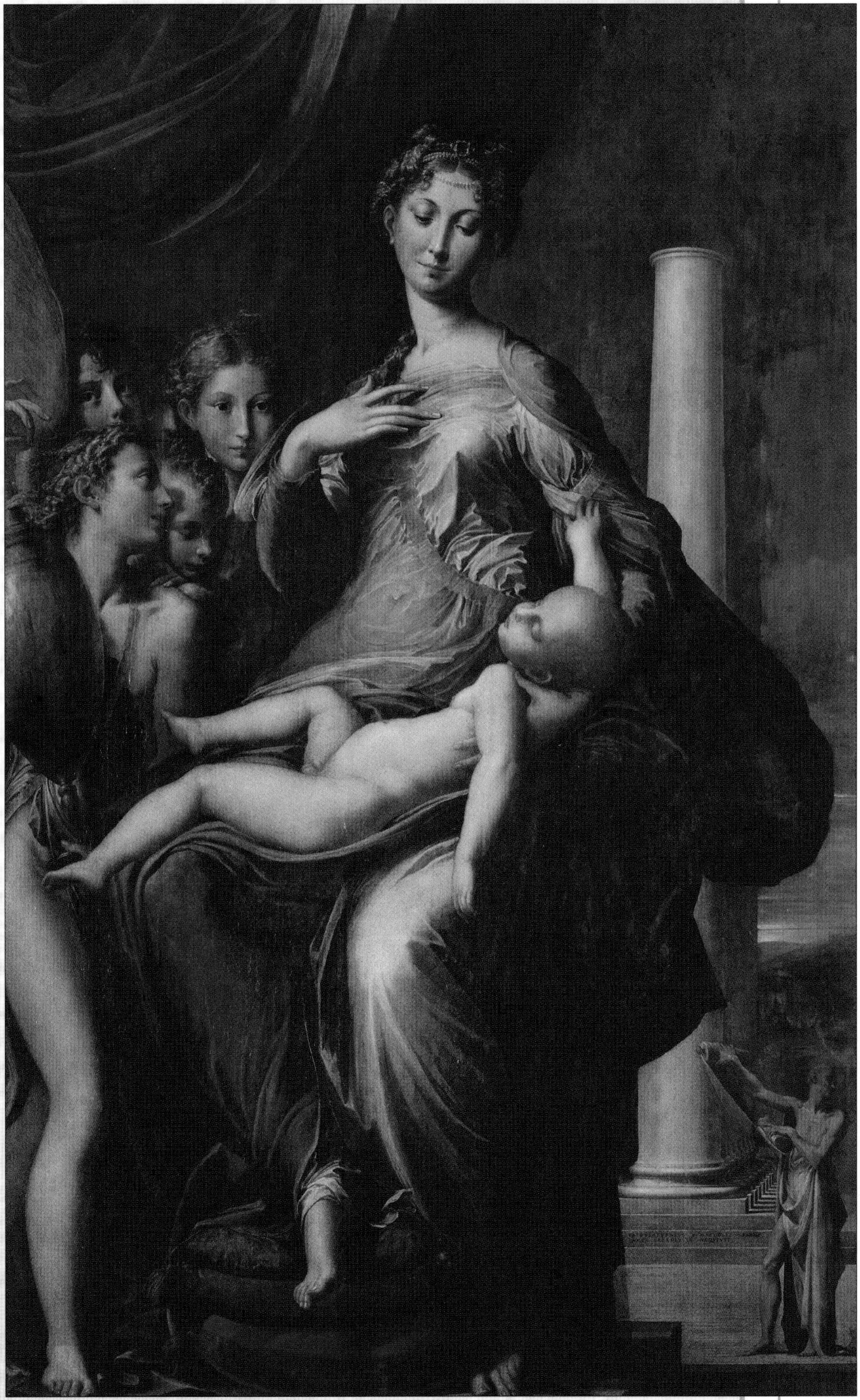

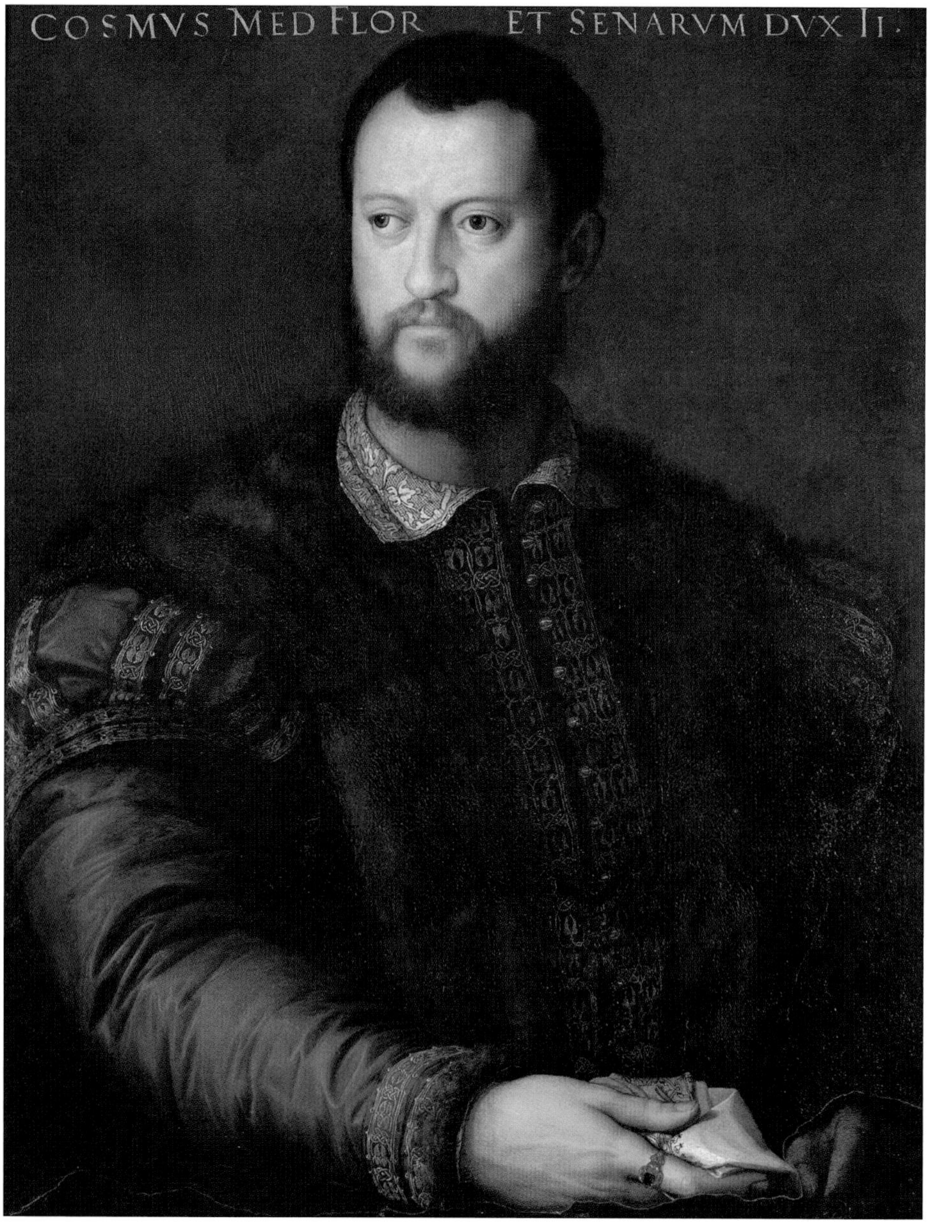

Bronzino's portrait of his patron, Cosimo I de' Medici (c.1545). Cosimo dressed in armor for the portrait, and the artist creates the impression of a detached, brooding, dangerous character.

Jacopo Pontormo (1494–1556), a sensitive, solitary artist whose contribution to the development of Mannerism was great. His picture of the *Madonna and Child with Saints*, completed in 1518, has been called the first Mannerist painting.

Another key work was *The Deposition from the Cross* (1525), featuring crowded figures picked out in bright colors as though lit by stage lights. Pontormo subsequently fell under the influence of Michelangelo, who became a personal friend.

Pontormo's closest artistic associate, however, was Agnolo Bronzino (1503–72), who started as his pupil and ended as his adopted son. Bronzino's talent was for portraiture, in which he pioneered a style of icy elegance that won him a post as court painter to Cosimo I de' Medici (1519–74), first grand duke of Tuscany. He gave his sitters an air of haughty refinement coupled, for the women, with a marblelike complexion that the French painter Ingres (1780–1867) would recapture three centuries later.

LEONARDO'S FOLLOWERS

The followers of Leonardo mostly took a gentler path than Michelangelo's tormented disciples. The Milanese painter Bernardino Luini (c.1480–1532) and the Sienese Giovanni Antonio Bazzi (1477–1549), known as Sodoma, both sought to capture the tenderness and grace of Leonardo's work but without his inspiration; the results seem dull and lifeless in comparison.

Sodoma's younger compatriot, Domenico Beccafumi (c.1485–1551), is rated more highly. His emotionally charged paintings feature the full range of Mannerist devices, including lurid lighting, extreme perspective effects, *contrapposto* poses, and *repoussoir* figures (in which objects at the side or in the foreground "push back" the main subject). Beccafumi is often called the last great Sienese painter.

CORREGGIO

Much more influential for the long term was the work of Antonio Allegri, known as Correggio (c.1490–1534) from his birthplace in the small town of that name. In 1510, aged about 21, he moved to Parma and spent the rest of his life there, working at a distance from the main Italian artistic centers.

Correggio developed Leonardo's *sfumato* technique to create a soft, dreamily sensuous style ideally suited for painting female nudes, his most successful theme. His masterpieces are a sequence of paintings illustrating the loves of the Roman god Jupiter, done for the Gonzaga dukes of Mantua, which were to have a profound effect on French 18th-century art.

Before that, Correggio had also done much to prefigure the Baroque style of the 17th century. He introduced a new way of using light and shade to balance forms and to direct the viewer's eye along predetermined lines. When combined with a daring use of

Toward the end of his life Correggio painted a series of mythological paintings including* Venus, Satyr, and Cupid *(c.1524–25). In these works the* sfumato *technique was well developed, as was his skill in painting fluent, luminous forms.

TOOLS AND TECHNIQUES

Chiaroscuro

The term chiaroscuro, meaning "light-dark," refers to the balance of light and shade in a picture and is generally used of those in which large dark areas predominate. Typical chiaroscuro effects are obtained by lighting the action by moonlight or candlelight, or by the miraculous glow given off by the infant Jesus or some holy object. The engraver Ugo da Carpi (c.1480–1532) made use of the device in wood prints drawn from the works of the Mannerist artist Parmigianino, and Correggio also featured it in such works as *The Holy Night* (1528–30) and *Judith* (1512–14).

perspective and a vigorous feeling for movement, this technique served to create works teeming with life, which seemed to predict the direction art would take 100 years or more after his own death in 1534.

THE VENETIAN SCHOOL

Correggio was an isolated prodigy, but 100 miles (160 km) to the east a whole school of painters was working through the Late Renaissance period to produce the finest body of work of the entire 16th century. Venice was spared the worst of the fighting in the Italian wars, and it retained its political independence to a greater degree than the other city-states.

Its rulers also kept the Counter-Reformation at arms' length, insisting for example that the Inquisition—an agency established by the Catholic church to suppress heresy—should operate in their territories only under close supervision.

As a result, the School of Venice, which had risen to maturity under Giovanni Bellini (1430–1516), continued to flourish. It took its direction from Giorgione (c.1477–1510), who had set the fashion for producing canvases for an elite of wealthy collectors willing to buy paintings for the sensual delight they afforded. If the Florentines were the masters of form, the Venetian masters were above all great colorists; their works glow with a multihued light.

TITIAN

Giorgione's most prominent heir was his friend and rival Tiziano Veccelli, known as Titian, who became official painter to the Republic of Venice on Bellini's death in 1516. From 1533 he was also court painter to Emperor Charles V (1500–58), the most powerful man in Europe at the time. In 1555, when Charles handed power to his son Philip II (1527–98), Titian kept his position. By that time he was about 70 years old and his reputation rivaled that of Michelangelo. Titian died in 1576, struck down by an epidemic of plague that also killed Orazio, his son and chief assistant. Legend has it that Titian was 99 years old at the time, although it seems more likely that he was in his early 90s.

Throughout his long career, Titian constantly renewed his talent, buoyed up on a seemingly inexhaustible fount of creative energy. Some characteristics remained constant throughout, notably the primacy of color. Titian followed Giorgione in softening the outlines of his figures and using light and shade to unify his compositions. The result was work that could express the private mood of the painter in a way that the stiffly formal works of Florentine painters such as Piero della Francesca (c.1415–92), for example, could not.

In his later years Titian's style loosened up even more. An assistant left

Titian's* Bacchus and Ariadne *(c.1522–23) contains striking examples of* contrapposto*. The poses of the two main characters—Bacchus, the god of wine, leaping from his chariot to declare his love for Ariadne (left)—convey the intense drama of the scene, which was inspired by the written accounts of classical authors such as Ovid and Catullus.

 See also: The High Renaissance in Italy 28–49

an intriguing description of his working method. He would sketch paintings rapidly in color, then leave them turned against the wall for months. Eventually he would revisit them, making repeated revisions and additions. In the last stages he would add much of the paint directly with his fingers, doing without a brush. The results were rich and radiant, the subjects dissolved in a bath of light.

The lesser Venetians

Titian may have dominated the Venetian School, but there were plenty of lesser talents to add their own contribution. Palma Vecchio (c.1480–1528) and Paris Bordone (?1500–71) both worked in a style similar to Titian's—in the latter case, so much so that experts still cannot agree whether certain works should be attributed to Bordone or to Titian.

Lorenzo Lotto (c.1480–1556/7) and Dosso Dossi (c.1490–1541/2) were eccentric individualists who learned from Bellini's feeling for landscape as well as Giorgione's taste for mythic subject matter. Lotto's work also showed the influence of German painting.

The artist Sebastiano del Piombo (c.1485–1547) started life as a close friend and associate of Titian. Later, he left Venice for Rome, where he came under the influence of Michelangelo and Raphael. He ended his life as a friar, stipulating in his will that he should be buried without ceremony so the money saved could be given to the poor.

One individual who stood apart from the mainstream of Venetian painting was Jacopo da Ponte (c.1515–92), known as Bassano for the provincial town where he lived. Bassano has been called the first populist painter. His canvases, often dealing with religious subjects, were peopled with peasants depicted energetically in thickly smeared paint with strong chiaroscuro effects. He also liked to introduce animals into his compositions, along with incidental still lifes of fruit, vegetables, and game.

Typical of Bassano's popular realism,* Jacob's Flight from Laban *(c.1570) contains lifelike detail of country people and animals.

Tintoretto

For sheer talent, none of the younger Venetians could match Jacopo Robusti (?1518–94). He was known as Tintoretto because his father was a *tintore* (dyer). Tintoretto's boast was that his work married Michelangelo's sense of design with Titian's skill with color. He brought all the drama and nervous energy of Mannerism into Venetian painting, favoring lopsided compositions based on strong diagonals, bathed in striking contrasts of light and shade.

His canvases were full of characters in violent movement, often seen from unexpected viewpoints and lit with a

Tintoretto's* Marriage at Cana *depicts Christ's first miracle (turning water into wine) with rich colors and bold brushstrokes.

flickering light. His contemporaries called him *Il Furioso* ("the furious one"), for his explosive creative energy. Sebastiano del Piombo, a slow worker, joked that Tintoretto could paint as much in two days as he could in two years.

Tintoretto's biographer Giorgio Vasari (1511–74) took him to task for the lack of finish in his paintings, claiming that he could have been one of the greatest of all masters if he had only taken more time over his works. But

TOOLS AND TECHNIQUES

Repoussoir

Derived from the French *repousser*, meaning "to push back," this term is applied to figures given prominence in the foreground, often to the side of a painting, that direct the viewer's eye to the center. They may take the form of people gesturing toward the main subject. The use of *repoussoir* was popular with the Mannerist artists of the mid-16th century and it broke with the High Renaissance tradition of symmetrical composition, introducing an unbalanced, dynamic element to pictorial design.

Veronese painted his controversial* The Feast in the House of Levi *for a monastery refectory. Beneath the grand arches of a portico the sumptuous banquet scene is filled with moving figures and humorous detail, suggesting a celebration of life itself.

Tintoretto preferred to work fast for immediacy and drama, even at the risk of seeming slipshod. A later painter, Annibale Carracci (1560–1609), remarked jokingly: "I have sometimes seen Tintoretto as equal to Titian and at other times as inferior to Tintoretto."

VERONESE

After Titian's death, Tintoretto's only real rival was Paolo Caliari (?1528–88), known as Veronese for the town of Verona where he was born. Veronese's specialty was huge paintings on biblical or historical themes, filled with gaily dressed crowds and beautiful, golden-haired women decked out in elegant clothes. He loved to depict feasts, preferably in splendid architectural settings. Commissioned to paint the ceilings of the Doge's Palace in Venice, he reveled in *sotto in sù* effects and complicated Mannerist poses.

Veronese's good-natured worldliness and gorgeous pageantry suited Venetian tastes but caused trouble with the Inquisition. In 1573 he was summoned to justify his painting of The Last Supper, which he had typically crowded with hordes of minor characters. When one inquisitor demanded "Does it seem fitting to you that at our Lord's last supper you should paint buffoons, drunkards, German soldiers, dwarfs, and similar indecencies?," Veronese replied: "We painters take liberties, like poets and people touched in the head."

Veronese was ordered to alter the work. Although unwilling, he eventually compromised by changing the title to *The Feast in the House of Levi*, the name by which the painting is still known today.

 See also: The Northern Renaissance **50–69**

By that time Venice too was beginning to feel the effects of the malaise afflicting the rest of Italy. The change in world trade routes had eaten away at the city's prosperity; in particular, the republic had lost its lucrative role as a middleman in the spice trade when the Portuguese started importing spices by sea directly from India. In 1573 Cyprus, a crucial trading base in the eastern Mediterranean, was lost to the Ottoman Turks. Painting also went into decline, and when Veronese and Tintoretto died in 1588 and 1594 respectively, there were no young artists of comparable stature to step into their shoes.

SCHOOLS AND MOVEMENTS

The Romanists

The name Romanists was given to the 16th-century Dutch and Flemish artists who looked to Italian painting and sculpture for inspiration. Many traveled to Italy, bringing back a zeal for the work of the great Renaissance masters and their Mannerist successors. Jan Gossaert (c.1478–1532), known as Mabuse, was one of the most influential figures in the development of the movement. He went to Italy in 1508. On his return to Antwerp, Mabuse introduced a new style of painting employing classical themes and ornate architectural settings. Other leading Romanists were Bernard van Orley (c.1490–1542), Maerten van Heemskerck (1498–1574), and Frans Floris (c.1519–70). By the mid-16th century, the influence of the Romanists was so great that an Italian trip had become a regular part of the apprenticeship of most Netherlandish painters.

THE NETHERLANDS

The situation in northern Europe was even less promising, as the religious strife set in motion by the Reformation was more violent there. The most prolific artistic center in Late Renaissance days was the Netherlands. Its primacy partly reflected an ongoing economic prosperity. Trade continued to flourish in Antwerp and other Flemish centers while Amsterdam was starting its rise in the Dutch provinces to the north.

For most of the century just two men ruled the country: Emperor Charles V until his abdication in 1555, and then his son, Philip II of Spain. Under the latter's rule, religious conflict took on a nationalist hue. Protestant revolt against Spanish Catholic rule broke out in 1563 and was put down by Philip's emissary, the duke of Alva, who governed oppressively between 1567 and 1573. The result was 40 years of strife that eventually ended with the division of the country between a Catholic south, still loyal to Spain, and the independent Protestant Dutch Republic in the north.

Before that time, however, Netherlandish artists benefited from the relative ease of travel within the emperors' domains to visit Italy. The result was the rise of the Romanist School (see box above). One of the most significant Flemish artists of the time even chose to make his career in Florence.

This was the sculptor Jean de Boulogne (1529–1608), or Giovanni da Bologna, often shortened to Giambologna. Trained in Flanders, he settled in Italy in about 1555 and subsequently became one of the leading Mannerist artists of his day.

PIETER BRUEGEL THE ELDER

Another, very different tradition also continued to flourish, one that had little in common with Italian fashions, even if its practitioners were prepared to borrow some Mannerist techniques. This was "genre" painting, devoted to portraying humble scenes of everyday life. Its practitioners included the north's greatest master of the time, Pieter Bruegel the Elder (c.1525–69), so called because he fathered a dynasty of painters, including two further generations of Pieters.

The elder Bruegel is sometimes referred to as "Peasant Bruegel" because he depicted peasant life in his works. Yet the nickname is misleading because, far from being a peasant himself, he was a townsman with a wicked satirical eye for the foibles and follies of the countryside.

Little is known of his life, except that he worked first in Antwerp and then in Brussels, where he was based in the 1560s when the duke of Alva unleashed his reign of terror. He also went to Italy as a young man, traveling as far south as Sicily and developing an enduring taste for the Italian landscape if not so much for the paintings he saw there.

MASTERPIECE

Bruegel's The Painter and the Connoisseur

Bruegel was about 40 when he drew this satirical self-portrait, entitled *The Painter and the Connoisseur*. In contrasting his own unkemptness with the smooth appearance of a bespectacled art lover, the Flemish master was making a point about the contrast between the creation of artworks and their acceptance by the art world. In his view, the painter has eyes only for his work. The connoisseur also contemplates it avidly while reaching for his wallet. Let us artists get on with our painting, Bruegel seems to say; we may need the money the art market brings, but we reserve the right to poke fun at those who provide for our needs.

Bruegel made few self-portraits. His pen-and-Ink drawing* The Painter and the Connoisseur *was intended as a satire on the art world.

When Bruegel returned to the Netherlands, he found his own unmistakable style, marked by the use of primary colors and an eye for the details of the way ordinary people lived. If he learned anything from his Italian contemporaries, it was in the way he composed his paintings, favoring the diagonal layouts dear to Mannerist hearts. For the most part, though, his tastes harked back to earlier northern masters such as Massys (c.1466–1530) and Bosch (c.1450–1516).

Like Bosch, Bruegel delighted in portraying people's foolishness and vices, although in a rather more amused and tolerant way. Yet he also had a poet's feeling for landscape, which he liked to paint from a high aerial perspective. He owes his greatness as an artist as much to the panoramic sweep of his settings as to his witty observations of human failings. In his combination of knowing humanity and grandiose vision, he was a worthy successor to the great masters of the preceding age.

***Hunters in the Snow** (c.1565) was one of a series of pictures based on the months of the year, painted by Bruegel for a wealthy merchant from Antwerp. He drew inspiration for the picture from the Swiss Alps, which he visited in the 1550s.*

MASTERPIECE

Michelangelo's The Last Judgment

In 1536, 24 years after he finished painting the ceiling of the Sistine Chapel in Rome (see pages 73 to 74), Michelangelo (1475–1564) started work on a fresh commission—to decorate the wall behind the chapel's high altar.

Times had changed in the intervening years, and the cultural horizon had darkened. Rome itself had been sacked by German forces of the Holy Roman Emperor in 1527. The Church had been split by the emergence of Protestantism in the northern lands. The Catholic reform movement called the Counter-Reformation was also getting underway. The Universal Inquisition would shortly be set up to combat heresy, while the Index of Prohibited Books listed condemned literary works.

Michelangelo signaled the new mood by choosing as his theme *The Last Judgment*, opting to put the mouth of Hell directly behind the central crucifix. He worked on the project for five years, and when the results were finally unveiled in 1541 they caused something of a scandal.

At the center of the painting is the figure of Christ. With his right hand raised, he forces the unfortunate figures on his left, who are trying to ascend, to fall down toward Hell. The chosen ones on his right are encouraged by the calm command of his left hand.

No one doubted Michelangelo's achievement, which marked the culmination of his study of the human figure; the wall served as an anthology of the human body at its most powerful, shown in every kind of contorted posture. The problem, in the newly censorious atmosphere of the Counter-Reformation, lay in the nudity of the figures.

The pope's Master of Ceremonies, Biagio de Casena, led a censorship campaign against the painting, expressing shock that naked bodies should be put on display in a sacred place. He declared that the work was better suited to the public baths or tavern than to a papal chapel. Michelangelo responded by painting Biagio's features onto the figure of the legendary king Minos, shown, complete with asses' ears, as the judge of Hell. The artist further indicated his feelings about the controversy by putting his own distorted face on the flayed skin clutched in the hand of the martyred Saint Bartholomew.

Despite the consternation it caused, the work was hugely influential and helped shape the future course of Mannerism. Yet the censors had the last laugh. In 1565 another artist, Daniele da Volterra (c.1509–66), was commissioned to paint loincloths over Michelangelo's figures. Ever since, Volterra—a friend of Michelangelo and a competent Mannerist painter in his own right—has been remembered in Italy as *il braghettone* ("the breeches-maker").

Michelangelo's The* Last Judgment*, from the altar wall of the Sistine Chapel in Rome (1541).

IONAS

Glossary

Words in SMALL CAPITALS refer to other entries in the glossary.

allegory image with an underlying meaning that is expressed symbolically.

altarpiece in Christian CHURCH ARCHITECTURE, a picture or decorated screen on or behind the altar. It may consist of a single painting or an elaborate group of hinged PANELS. *See also* DIPTYCH; TRIPTYCH.

architecture 1 science or art of building. 2 the structure or STYLE of what is built.

baptistery place where baptism is performed in CHURCH.

baroque 1 STYLE of ARCHITECTURE, painting, and sculpture originating principally in Italy, of the late 16th to early 18th centuries; it exhibited an increased interest in dynamic movement and dramatic effects. The style reached its peak in c.1625–75, when it became known as High Baroque. 2 overelaborate, florid. 3 period in the 17th century when the baroque style was at its height.

basilica MEDIEVAL CHURCH in which the nave is taller than the aisles.

Book of Hours book of prayers to be said at canonical hours, used privately by people in their homes.

brushstroke individual mark made by each application of paint with a brush, usually retaining the mark of the separate brush hairs.

bust portrait sculpture showing the sitter's head and shoulders only.

Byzantine art art of the eastern Roman Empire centered on Constantinople (formerly known as Byzantium, now Istanbul, Turkey) from the 4th century C.E.

chiaroscuro ("light-dark") pictorial use of light and shade to convey shadow and highlight three-dimensional form.

church 1 building designed for Christian worship. The first churches were based on the Roman BASILICA. 2 the whole body of Christian believers.

classic 1 the finest art of its kind in any given period. 2 Greek art and ARCHITECTURE of the 5th century B.C.E. 3 art of the Roman and Greek antique world. 4 art that adheres to high standards of craftsmanship, PROPORTION, symmetry, and logic.

classical synonymous with CLASSIC (2, 3, and 4).

colorist artist who specializes in, or is famed for his or her use of color.

commission 1 a work of art ordered by a PATRON. 2 contract to produce work for a patron.

composition the way in which something (e.g., a painting) is visually arranged or put together.

contrapposto posing of the human form in painting or sculpture so that the head and shoulders are twisted in a different direction from hips and legs.

copperplate a copper plate on which a design is etched or engraved.

Counter-Reformation religious movement in the form of a Catholic revival, which began in direct opposition to the Protestant Reformation sweeping across Europe in the mid-16th century. *See also* REFORMATION.

Cubism artistic movement c.1907–20 initiated by Pablo Picasso and Georges Braque. Cubism aimed to analyze FORMS in geometric terms or reorganize them in various contexts; color remained secondary to form.

devotional associated with, or the object of, religious worship.

diptych pair of painted or sculptured PANELS, hinged or joined together; especially popular for DEVOTIONAL pictures in the MIDDLE AGES. *See also* ALTARPIECE.

draftsmanship skill in drawing or plan-making.

drapery the arrangement of folds of material, painted or sculpted.

Early Renaissance *See* RENAISSANCE.

engraving 1 the technique of incising lines on wood, or types of metal such as copper. *See also* MEZZOTINT. 2 the impression made from the engraved block.

Expressionism in its widest sense, describes work in which artists are more concerned to express human emotions than to depict reality. (Also, **Expressionist.**)

figuration 1 FORM, shape. 2 ornamentation with design. 3 depiction of figures, especially human.

figurative 1 representational. 2 metaphorical, not literal.

figurative art art depicting recognizable figures or objects; synonymous with REPRESENTATIONAL ART.

figure drawing (and figure painting) drawing or painting in which the human figure predominates, usually full-length.

foreground in painting or drawing, the PLANE nearest the viewer.

foreshortening the use of the laws of PERSPECTIVE in art to make an individual FORM appear three-dimensional.

form the shape or appearance the artist gives his subject.

fresco ("fresh") MURAL painting on fresh plaster.

genre painting type of painting depicting daily life, popularized by 17th-century Dutch painters such as Vermeer.

gesso generally used for the mixture of any inert white

PIGMENT (such as plaster of Paris, chalk, or gypsum) with glue; strictly, a mixture in which the inert pigment is calcium sulfate. The mixture was used to cover smooth surfaces such as wood, stone, or canvas, and provide a ground for painting.

gilding the coating of a surface with GOLD LEAF. (Also, **gilded**.)

gilt silver or other metal decorated with GOLD LEAF.

glaze 1 transparent layer of paint applied over another; light passes through and is reflected back, modifying or intensifying the underlayer. 2 vitreous layer made from silica, applied to pottery as decoration or to make it watertight.

golden section system of PROPORTION dating from antiquity and originally thought to have harmonious aesthetic qualities. Usually expressed as a straight line divided into two unequal parts; the shorter length bears the same relation to the longer as the longer does to the whole.

gold leaf gold beaten into a thin sheet. *See also* GILDING.

Gothic the last period of MEDIEVAL art and ARCHITECTURE. Early Gothic usually refers to the period 1140 to 1200; High Gothic c.1200 to 1250; late Gothic from 1250. It is mainly characterized as an architectural STYLE, but also by the sculpture, painting, and ornament of the period in which the architecture was built. "Gothic" was used in the RENAISSANCE as an adjective to condemn the "medieval" style.

guild MEDIEVAL form of professional association that regulated standards of craftsmanship and commercial activity.

high art art that strives to attain the highest aesthetic and moral qualities in both content and expression.

High Renaissance *See* RENAISSANCE.

icon in BYZANTINE, Russian, and Greek Orthodox CHURCH art, a representation of Christ or the Virgin, or saints, executed either in MOSAIC or painting; tending to be stereotyped, or in a STYLE following certain fixed types and methods. (Also, **iconic**.)

imagery representation of images or forms in art; putting into paint an artist's mental picture of something.

inlay the decoration of furniture, pottery, metalwork, etc., by inserting patterns of wood, stone, or shell into the body of the object so that the surface remains level.

International Gothic courtly STYLE in painting, sculpture, and the decorative arts that was prevalent in western Europe, particularly France, northern Italy, and the Netherlands from c.1375–1425. The style balanced the naturalistic and the idealistic, and was characterized by delicate and rich coloring.

linear perspective method of indicating spatial RECESSION in a picture by placing objects in a series of receding PLANES; parallel lines (orthogonals) receding from the onlooker's viewpoint appear to meet at a VANISHING POINT.

low relief *See* RELIEF.

mannered the exaggerated characteristics of any STYLE.

Mannerism artistic STYLE originating in Italy c.1520–90 (between HIGH RENAISSANCE and BAROQUE) tending to employ distorted POSES, elongated human figures, artificial and brash color, and a highly charged emotional content. (Also, **Mannerist**; **mannered**.)

master in the MEDIEVAL GUILD system, one who was sufficiently skilled to be able to practice his art on his own.

masterpiece originally the name given to a test piece of work done by the MEDIEVAL apprentice in order to qualify as a MASTER of his GUILD. The term is now used more freely to mean an artist's work of outstanding importance or quality.

medieval *See* MIDDLE AGES.

medium 1 the means through which an artist expresses him- or herself, e.g., painting, sculpture, etc. 2 the materials an artist uses, e.g. in sculpture: metal, marble, etc. 3 the substance with which PIGMENT is mixed and thinned to make paint, e.g., egg yolk to produce egg TEMPERA, linseed oil to produce oil paint, etc.

mezzotint 1 method of copper ENGRAVING. 2 print produced by this method.

Middle Ages in European history, the period between the end of classical antiquity and the start of the RENAISSANCE, 4th–15th century C.E. (Also, **medieval**.)

miniature very small piece of work. During the RENAISSANCE and the 18th and 19th centuries the term was often applied to small portraits painted on ivory.

mosaic design formed from small pieces of stone, glass, marble, etc.

mural picture painted on a wall or ceiling.

mythological painting painting of subjects chosen from classical mythology, popular from the 15th to the 19th centuries, e.g., *Primavera* (c.1482) by Sandro Botticelli.

naturalism accurate, detailed representation of objects or scenes as they appear, whether attractive or otherwise. *See also* REALISM.

palette 1 piece of wood, metal, or glass on which an artist mixes paint. 2 range of colors used by the artist.

panel 1 flat piece of wood or metal used as a painting support, as distinct from a canvas. 2 distinct area or compartment as part of a design, as on an ALTARPIECE.

patron someone who patronizes or supports the arts and artists.

perspective method of representing objects on a two-dimensional surface so that they appear three-dimensional. *See also* LINEAR PERSPECTIVE.

Pietà representation of the Virgin Mary holding the dead body of Christ.

pigment a colored solid, usually dispersed in a MEDIUM to form paint.

plane in art, a predominantly flat surface.

portal imposing entrance of a building.

portrait a drawn or painted image of a person, usually one that is naturalistic and identifiable. (Also, **portraiture**; **portraitist**.)

pose the stance or attitude of the human figure, or group of figures, in a painting or sculpture.

Pre-Raphaelite Brotherhood English association of artists that flourished in the mid-19th century. It included Dante Gabriel Rossetti, William Holman Hunt, and John Everett Millais. They shared a desire to breathe new life into artistic traditions, and an admiration of Italian art "pre-Raphael," i.e., before the HIGH RENAISSANCE. They were inspired by the sincerity of such art, using it as a guide for studying nature directly, and for creating images with a genuine moral content.

proportion ratio or relationship of dimensions. *See also* GOLDEN SECTION.

Quattrocento 15th century.

Realism 1 in art, similar to NATURALISM in attempting to convey subjects accurately. (Also, **Realist**.) 2 a STYLE of painting dating from the 19th century, typified by Gustave Courbet, that deliberately depicts everyday subject matter.

recession in painting, the illusion of depth or distance achieved through the use of color or PERSPECTIVE.

Reformation a religious movement in 16th-century Europe that sought to modify aspects of Roman Catholic teaching and practice and to establish Protestant CHURCHES. *See also* COUNTER-REFORMATION.

relief sculpture, carving, etc., in which forms project from a background PLANE, and depth is hollowed out of that plane; the type of relief is determined by the degree to which the design stands out; thus *alto rilievo* (high relief") and *basso rilievo*, or *bas relief* ("low relief"), in which the projection is slight.

Renaissance ("rebirth") the period of Italian art from c.1400–1525, characterized by increased emphasis on accurate depiction of the natural world, and the rediscovery of classical art. The EARLY RENAISSANCE is deemed to be between c.1420 and 1450; HIGH RENAISSANCE refers to the period of the finest achievements of Leonardo da Vinci, Raphael, and Michelangelo Buonarroti, c.1450–1525.

representational art art that attempts to show objects as they really appear, or at least in some easily recognizable form. Synonymous with FIGURATIVE ART.

Romanticism art movement of the late 18th and early 19th centuries, in which literary themes and the imagination of the artist predominated.

sacra conversazione ("sacred conversation") the image of the Virgin and Child with saints, as a group portrait.

sfumato ("shaded") using subtle gradations of TONE and softened lines.

statuary collection of statues, or the making of statues.

still life painting of inanimate objects, such as fruit, flowers, dead game (rabbits, deer, fish, pheasants, etc.).

style manner of artistic expression, particular to an individual school or period.

stylized 1 conforming to a recognized STYLE. 2 based on natural forms that are then simplified according to a conventional stereotype.

symbol image of something representing something else. (Also, **symbolic**; **symbolize**.)

tempera (or egg tempera) technique of painting in which egg or egg yolk is blended into PIGMENT and used as a MEDIUM; before the late 15th century it was the most common medium used on PANEL paintings.

terra-cotta ("baked earth") hard, fired, unglazed brown-red clay used for pottery, sculpture, and building.

tone 1 atmosphere, character. 2 intensity of color or hue. 3 degree of lightness or darkness.

Trinità representation of the Holy Trinity: the Father, the Son, and the Holy Ghost.

triptych picture or carving in three parts; commonly seen as ALTARPIECES.

vanishing point point at which the receding parallel lines in a painting appear to meet. *See* LINEAR PERSPECTIVE; FORESHORTENING.

virtuosity special skill of execution.

woodblock *See* WOODCUT.

woodcut a design cut to stand out in RELIEF from a woodblock; a print made from a woodblock.

wood engraving a design engraved with a burin (engraver's tool) on hardwood. The printing method is as for the WOODCUT.

workshop place in which art objects or paintings are executed. "Workshop" work is usually not by the MASTER but by his assistants.

Further References

General

Jardine, Lisa, *Worldly Goods: A New History of the Renaissance*, W. W. Norton, New York and London, 1998.

Johnson, Geraldine A., *Renaissance Art: A Very Short Introduction*, Oxford University Press, Oxford, UK, 2005.

Strauss-Art, Suzanne, *The Story of the Renaissance*, Pemblewick Press, Lincoln, MA, 1997.

In-Depth Books

Adams, Laurie Schneider, *Italian Renaissance Art*, Westview Press, Boulder, CO, 2001.

Clark, Kenneth, *Leonardo da Vinci* (revised edn.), Penguin Books, Harmondsworth, UK, 1989.

Dixon, Laurinda, *Bosch*, Phaidon Press, New York, 2003.

Gibson, Walter S., *Bruegel*, Thames & Hudson, London/Oxford University Press, New York, 1977; reprinted 2002.

Goffen, Rona, *Renaissance Rivals: Michelangelo, Leonardo, Raphael, Titian*, Yale University Press, New Haven, CT, 2004.

Harbison, Craig, *The Mirror of the Artist: Northern Renaissance Art*, Prentice Hall, Upper Saddle River, NJ, 2003.

Hartt, Frederick, and David G. Wilkins, *History of Italian Renaissance Art*, Prentice Hall Art, Englewood Cliffs, NJ, 2006.

Hibbard, Howard, *Michelangelo*, HarperCollins, New York, 1985.

Huyghe, René (ed.), *The Larousse Encyclopedia of Renaissance and Baroque Art*, Bookthrift Co., New York, 1985.

Jones, Roger, and Nicholas Penny, *Raphael*, Yale University Press, New Haven, CT, 1987.

Kemp, Martin, *Leonardo*, Oxford University Press, New York, 2004.

King, Ross, *Michelangelo and the Pope's Ceiling* (new edn.), Pimlico, London, 2006.

Murray, Peter, and Linda Murray, *The Art of the Renaissance*, Thames & Hudson, London, 1999.

Paoletti, John T., and Gary M. Radke, *Art in Renaissance Italy* (3rd edn.), Prentice Hall, Upper Saddle River, NJ, 2006.

Roberts-Jones, Philippe, *Pieter Bruegel*, Harry N. Abrams, New York, 2002.

Smith, Jeffrey Chipps, *The Northern Renaissance*, Phaidon Press, London, 2004.

Snyder, James, *The Northern Renaissance*, Prentice Hall, Upper Saddle River, NJ, 2004.

Welch, Evelyn, *Art in Renaissance Italy: 1350–1500*, Oxford University Press, Oxford, UK, 2001.

Classics

Berenson, Bernhard, *The Italian Painters of the Renaissance*, Ursus Press, New York, 1998.

Burckhardt, Jacob, *The Civilization of the Renaissance in Italy*, Penguin Classics, Harmondsworth, UK, 1990.

Cellini, Benvenuto, *The Autobiography of Benvenuto Cellini*, Penguin Classics, Harmondsworth, UK, 1999.

Vasari, Giorgio, *Lives of the Artists* (Oxford World's Classics series), Oxford University Press, Oxford, UK, 1998.

Web Sites

www.wsu.edu:8080/~dee/REN/IDEA.HTM
The Idea of the Renaissance: part of a World Civilizations resource from Washington State University.

www.all-art.org/history214_contents_Renaissance.html
Part of the World History of Art Web site, providing basic information on individual artists and a selection of their works.

www.renaissanceconnection.org/main.cfm
An interactive site developed by the Education Department of the Allentown Art Museum in Pennsylvania.

www.abcgallery.com/
Provides access to Olga's Gallery, one of the largest online art collections. Use the index to find the artists you want—the site will provide a selection of their works.

www.wga.hu/
The Web Gallery of Art also provides access to a comprehensive selection of Renaissance paintings.

http://witcombe.sbc.edu/ARTHrenaissanceitaly.html
A comprehensive art history site provided by a professor at Sweet Briar College, VA.

Index

Page numbers in *italics* refer to illustrations, and page numbers in brackets indicate a box feature. Bold type denotes chapter headings, and underlined numbers indicate a topic's major treatment in the volume.

A

B

C

D

E

F

G

H

I

J

L

M

N

O

P

Q

R

Picture Credits

AKG 9, 23, 26/247, 41, 43, 44, 58, 59, 62, 65, 66, 69, 86; **Pietro Baguzzi** 75; **Orsi Battaglini** 75; **Cameraphoto** 14, 37, 82, 83; **Electa** 15, 34, 39, 45, 78. 89; **Erich Lessing** 12/13, 20, 24, 25, 32, 33, 36, 38, 47, 50, 52, 55, 60, 61, 63, 64, 72, 72/73, 77, 79, 81, 87; **Paul M.R. Maeyaert** 54; **Rabatti-Domingie** 11, 18, 19, 21, 29, 30/31, 46, 49, 57, 70, 76, 84; **Shutterstock: Danilo Ascione** 3

The Brown Reference Group has made every effort to trace copyright holders of the pictures used in this book. Anyone having claims to ownership not identified above is invited to contact The Brown Reference Group.